PINK RIBBON
Adventure

*Amazing Works of God in the
Midst of Breast Cancer*

MARCIA DeVRIES

With Dave DeVries and Hannah DeVries

WESTBOW
PRESS®
A DIVISION OF THOMAS NELSON
& ZONDERVAN

WestBow Press books may be ordered through booksellers or by contacting:

WestBow Press
A Division of Thomas Nelson & Zondervan
1663 Liberty Drive
Bloomington, IN 47403
www.westbowpress.com
1 (866) 928-1240

ISBN: 978-1-5127-5584-8 (sc)
ISBN: 978-1-5127-5585-5 (hc)
ISBN: 978-1-5127-5583-1 (e)

Library of Congress Control Number: 2016914685

Print information available on the last page.

WestBow Press rev. date: 10/27/2016

Dedication

This book is dedicated to my Lord and Savior Jesus Christ. He alone is the author; I am merely the scribe. May all who read this book see His deep love for us and His awesome power which is available to everyone. Praise You, Jesus. You are good, all the time.

Contents

Introduction

Dear reader,

Are you going through the wilderness of cancer? Are you scared? Angry? Discouraged? Dreading the future? Feeling all alone? Are you trying to figure out why God has allowed this trial to enter your life?

Pink Ribbon Adventure is our true story that shows what God can do in the midst of breast cancer. We did not ask for cancer, but when we entered this deep valley where the shadow of death was lurking, God was there with us every step of the way. He walked so closely with us and provided everything we needed, from tangible help to emotional help.

In this book my husband Dave, our daughter Hannah and I share amazing stories from our lives that show how God worked miraculously during this struggle to beat breast cancer. After all the surgeries and treatments were over, we were able to look back and honestly say that having cancer was a priceless gift from God. We learned many lessons and grew so much closer to the Lord and to each other.

Did we do everything right? No. In fact, I think this book should have been called "The Good, The Bad, and The Ugly." It shows our failures as well as God's blessings. We were learning all the way through this wilderness, and are still learning.

This cancer adventure was like a roller coaster ride; it had exhilarating highs and lows. We saw God do amazing things that left us in awe, but we also saw God perform painful open heart surgery on our hearts. Both were needed and beautiful.

Hang on, dear friend. God will meet you right where you are. Call out to Him. He wants to pour out blessings on you, too. May He send you encouragement and hope, just as He did to us.

Blessings!
Marcia DeVries

A Special Gift

It was October 2012, and my husband, Dave, and I were in Riviera Maya, Mexico celebrating our 25th wedding anniversary. It was a trip of a lifetime for us, since neither of us had ever been on a luxury trip before. We had a wonderful time at an all inclusive resort. The weather was perfect, and the scenery was gorgeous. We snorkeled, toured ancient Mayan ruins, swam in the beautiful ocean, and ate delicious food. This trip was all that we had hoped for as we celebrated 25 wonderful years of marriage. This was a special gift from God, because our lives were just about to be turned up-side down.

The Adventure Begins

Marcia:

It was now January 2013, and my husband (Dave) and I were in the doctor's office hearing the words, "You have breast cancer." *Instantly* the Lord brought back to my mind a lesson I had learned over 30 years ago. Because of this lesson, I just *knew* that really good things were going to come out of this trial. After leaving the doctor's office, I felt like I was floating down the hallway. I had a sense of excitement, like we were just about to start a new adventure. I couldn't wait! How crazy is that?

Let me share with you what this important lesson was.

An Important Lesson

Marcia:

This story really began in 1980 when I was fifteen years old. A life changing event was about to happen to me that would prepare me well for the huge trial of cancer that God would send to me in the future. It was summertime, and I wanted to get my driver's license right on my sixteenth birthday in August. In order for this to happen, I was taking driver's ed. during summer school.

One day when my mom picked me up from driver's ed., she told me that she wouldn't be able to pick me up the following week. She had found a lump in her abdomen and was going to have surgery to remove it. Back then, in order to know what was going on, they did "exploratory" surgery.

The day of the surgery came, and my dad came home from the hospital and called all four of us kids to the kitchen table. He told us that the doctor had found extensive ovarian cancer. The doctor removed all that he could, but it was spread everywhere like sand, and he couldn't remove it all. Then my dad broke down sobbing. It was like a bomb had just gone off. Eventually we all drifted off to other parts of the house.

I went up to the bedroom that I shared with my sister, and as I sat there alone on my bed, I cried until I had no more tears to cry. Then as I sat there in silence, for the first time in my life, I heard the Lord speak to me. This was not an audible voice, but in my heart I sensed that He was asking me if I was going to get angry with Him and become bitter, or if I was going to trust Him. I thought about it for a while, and then said, "Lord, I will trust you." Then an amazing thing happened. The Bible came alive to me! This was the first time that I heard the Lord speak directly to *me*. I began to grow spiritually at a rapid pace. Verses nearly jumped off the page at me when I read the Bible.

In those days they didn't know how to control the side effects of chemo therapy very well, and it hurt so much to watch my mom suffer with these ravaging side effects. I remember riding the bus to school and turning my head toward the window to hide my tears. God comforted me again and again with many verses. He sent me verses like: Psalms 112:7 "They will have no fear of bad news; their hearts are steadfast, trusting in the LORD." (NIV) It felt like God was wrapping His arms around me and wiping away my tears.

The Lord became my rock during this time. I pictured Him as my huge rock, unmovable, unchangeable, always there for me. I took comfort in the fact that He would never get sick and die. Verses like Psalm 18:2 meant so much to me. "The LORD is my *rock* and my fortress and my deliverer, my God, my *rock*, in whom I take refuge; my shield and the horn of my salvation, my strong hold." (NASB)

It was during this time that my faith in God became *my* faith, not just my parents'. I was no longer going through the motions, riding along on their coat tails. I now owned my faith in God.

My mom died three and a half years later during Christmas break of my freshman year in college. I look back on my mom's illness as a precious gift from God because, though I never would have chosen to have my mom get sick and die, God used her illness to wake me up and mature me spiritually. I learned that God was not some distant God who created me and then said--ok, you're on your own now. He loved me and wanted to be involved in each day of my life. A very important lesson that God taught me through all this is that hard times can bring really good things. Ever since then, I haven't dreaded trials, because I know that *trials can bring treasures*. Little did I know how important that lesson would be to me in the future.

On the Threshhold

Dave:

As I sat in the waiting room with Jim Carlson, our interim pastor, I knew it was cancer. Marcia had felt a lump in her breast in late November, and the subsequent testing led us to have the suspicious lump removed in January 2013 at our local hospital.

In the short time that I knew Jim, he proved to be a close friend. He had the ability to be compassionate, caring, and encouraging all at the same time. He was someone that God had put into my life at just the right time.

After the surgery, the doctor talked to both myself and Jim. Lab tests had yet to be done on the lump that was removed, so the doctor could not say anything conclusive. Afterwards, Jim asked me, "What did you hear the doctor say?" I said, "I heard him say it's cancer." Jim replied, "So did I." A few days later, the lab results confirmed it. My wife had breast cancer.

In Sickness or in Health

Dave:

Let me go back a number of years to bring you to this point in my life. When I was eighteen and in my freshman year of college, my mother contracted a rare degenerative brain disease called Creutzfeldt Jakob Disease (CJD). To some, the symptoms of this disease may seem similar to Alzheimer's disease.

Almost six years later, my mom passed away. Although she lingered on this earth until I was twenty four, I feel like I lost her at age ninteen, because that is when she lost the ability to communicate. I watched my father love and care for her even when she could give nothing back to him. It was a great example to me as a young man.

When I met Marcia, she also had experienced the premature death of her mother, and had watched her dad lovingly care for her mom also. These shared experiences are part of what brought us together as we began dating during my senior year of college.

Because of the model of selfless love my dad showed to my mom, I knew I had to show this same kind of love to Marcia. When I married Marcia in 1987, I was binding myself to a life of commitment for better or for worse, for richer or for poorer, in sickness and in health. However, when you are young, these things seem a long way off.

As we grew older and had children who were approaching their college years, a thought kept creeping into my mind. We were quickly approaching the same time of life in which Marcia had lost her mom, and I had lost my mom. Could this happen to us? Would I be asked to endure what both my father and father-in-law went through? I prayed that I would not, but felt as though in some way I would experience this in one shape or form. As our children entered college, each year I'd hold my breath. Each year I was thankful for another year with Marcia.

An Example to Follow

Dave:

Back in the mid 1990's, we first discovered a lump in one of Marcia's breasts. We obviously were alarmed, but after tests were done, it was found that it was only a harmless fluid filled cyst. Over the years, she had a number of these cysts. It came to the point where they seemed somewhat routine. However, when Marcia felt the lump in November of 2012, it felt different. I still was not overly concerned, but we proceeded to have it checked out anyway.

Just before Christmas, Carrie Gaul, a long time friend of ours, stopped in to visit us. She and her husband Dennis had moved away from our town a few years before to pursue a ministry to which God had called them to. She was now back in town visiting family and friends and stopped in to see us. It was great catching up with her especially since she had been diagnosed with breast cancer that previous year. We had been praying for her over the past year and kept up with her progress on Facebook and email.

Now, however, we were getting her story up close and in person. Her visit confirmed what we sensed. God had been taking her and her husband on an amazing journey of trusting God and seeing Him work in their lives. It was so encouraging to hear, and we praised God with her. As we visited and heard Carrie testify to God's goodness, grace, and amazing work in their lives, two things came to my mind.

First, I thought that I had never before seen a person handle the disease of cancer in this way. "This is the way it should be," I thought. One should look at this challenge in life as a gift from God, to see Him work in your life and the lives of your family members in amazing ways that would not happen unless you walked this path. I thought, "If we ever have to go through something like this in our lives, I want to handle it in the same way that they have." Then I heard the Holy Spirit whisper into my heart that I was next.

My second thought was that God was using this very conversation with Carrie to prepare me for this very same cancer journey. At the time, nothing was yet conclusive from Marcia's tests. She was scheduled for a breast MRI in a few days, but in my heart, I already knew that this was cancer.

God, however, was graciously preparing me for what was ahead. This was not just a warning. Instead, it was an encouragement to live my life in such a way as to glorify God in the midst of trials.

Our daughter Hannah was with us that day when Carrie stopped by, and she later told me that God also used this conversation to prepare her for what was ahead as well. God always gives us what we need when we need it. All the praise and glory goes to Him.

Growing Up with Fear

Hannah:

Everyone has fears while growing up. As a kid you tend to be afraid of the dark, monsters under the bed, or being kidnapped. There are all manner of fears that can take hold of you, and if left unchecked, can consume your life. When I was growing up I was afraid of the dark like many kids, but my biggest fear was losing my parents. I have been blessed to have a wonderful relationship with the most supportive and loving parents. They taught me to love the Lord with all my heart, and have supported me in all my endeavors.

At summer camp when I was sixteen, I remember giving my parents up into the Lord's hands because I recognized what a hold that fear held on my life. I was not trusting God with my parent's lives. After that moment my fear subsided quite a bit, but was never fully gone.

As I got older, my mom told me about how her mom had died. Her mom had been diagnosed with ovarian cancer when she was fifteen, and she passed away when my mom was a freshman in college.

As I approached *my* freshman year of college, my fear of losing my mom niggled in the back of my mind. I knew this fear was irrational because of the hope I had in Christ, but I still felt it all throughout that year. My freshman year came and went, as did the first half of my sophomore year. During this time I unconsciously heaved a sigh of relief that mom was still here and that I wouldn't lose her like she lost her mom.

An Uneasy Feeling

Hannah:

Around Christmastime of 2012, Mom told me that she had found a lump in her breast and was going to get it checked out. This wasn't abnormal as she would get cysts from time to time. It wasn't a big deal, but as the weeks passed, they kept running more tests because it wasn't normal. I went back to school after telling my parents to keep me updated on every step. If she did have cancer, I didn't want to be surprised by it. As all of the tests went on, I just had this feeling that she was going to test positive for cancer.

Journal Entry: January 27, 2013

> *"Truthfully, the thought of Mom having cancer, and the further thought of her dying just makes my heart clench in pain. I cannot begin to express how much I love my mom and how thankful I am for her. I have been so blessed to have had her around for the past two years, mostly because I'm continually reminded of the fact that her mom died of cancer her freshman year of college, and was sick even before that. In the past year I have had so many wonderful conversations with her, and she has given me so much good advice. I've been blessed to give her some as well. I've been able to know my parents and get close to them as adults, something neither of my parents were able to do with their moms*

since they both died early. The future is uncertain, and I am already fearful and hurting, but God, no matter what the outcome of all this is... "I WILL STILL PRAISE YOU." Psalm 103.

Preparing Our Kids

Marcia:

One of the hardest things we had to do was call our kids in college and tell them that I had breast cancer. I wish we could have told them in person, but they were both over ten hours away. We were soon blown away at how well God had already planned to ease the blow.

Our son, Jonathan, was going to college in Texas at LeTourneau University. We didn't know this, but two weeks earlier, his close friend and roommate had just learned that *his* mom had breast cancer. Now they could go through this trial together. One of Jonathan's professors always began the class (that they were both taking) by asking how the moms were doing. Then he would stop and pray for us. This brings tears to my eyes even now.

Our daughter, Hannah, was going to college in Mississippi at Mississippi College. The night that we called her with the news, it was terrible timing. She had fifteen minutes to get to the cafeteria to eat dinner, race over to an evening class that only met once a week, and then go to her Christian social club meeting.

On her way to this meeting, she ran into a friend who was going to a different social club meeting and told her the news. There, at her friend's meeting, all of the girls stopped and prayed for Hannah and for all of us.

When Hannah went to her own meeting, one girl read a very sweet, touching, encouraging message she had written about Hannah. She had no idea that Hannah had just received bad news from home. Then when Hannah shared the news, they all came around her, laid hands on her, and prayed for her and for us. Then, the next evening she went to church where she shared it again. Hannah said that within twenty-four hours, about 250 people had prayed for us all. God was already helping our kids through this trial.

Excited?

Hannah:

Journal Entry: January 28, 2013

"I feel like I could write a book about my mom and how much she has taught me over the past year, but right now I'll just stick to what she told me today. I'm literally astounded by her attitude toward all of this. The other day she was telling me about how all things are a gift from God, and how trials are gifts. She told me she was excited about going through this trial… excited. She is excited to see what the Lord will do through all of this, what he teaches her, and how much she will grow in her relationship with Him. Today she told me that she doesn't like the word 'journey.' She told me that in her mind this is not a journey, but an adventure, and she is so looking forward to starting this spiritual adventure. What an example. I am clinging to the Lord for my strength, but her attitude and example are a huge reason I haven't already dissolved into a puddle. The Lord will teach us through all this, and no matter what, He is faithful. "Bless the Lord, o my soul, and all that is within me, bless His holy name. Bless the Lord, o my soul, and forget not all his benefits. Psalms 103:1-2" (ESV)

The Diagnosis

Hannah:

It was on a Tuesday night in January, right before I went to class, when my parents called me to tell me that mom had been diagnosed with breast cancer. Then I went to a class that I can't remember a word of. I knew she wasn't in immediate danger of dying, but there are no words to express what a daughter feels when she finds out that her mom has cancer. Her cancer was a fast growing cancer, and suddenly the possibility of her dying became a reality. Immediately my fears rushed back in my face. Within weeks she would be having a mastectomy and soon after would begin chemotherapy.

Journal Entry: January 31, 2013

"On Tuesday, January 29th, 2013, at 5:15 p.m., I found out that my mom has breast cancer. I know we've been preparing for this possibility for a few weeks now, but now it's here. It's real. It hurts. But…it's good. I won't deny that it hurts my heart that she will have a mastectomy next week, that the thought of her dying rips me up inside, and the fact that I am twelve hours away from her during all this. It is all so difficult for me to bear; and yet, Lord, You have yet to give me any reason why I could not trust You. You have always provided for us and sustained us. Why should I stop trusting You now? I surely will not. You have paved the way for me to have an incredible support system of

eight different groups while I am here at school. See how good God is?! Try to tell me He's not. I dare you. Thought so. I'll never deny that this is super hard for me, but God has granted me a strength and joy beyond what this earth can throw at me. God has already used this whole situation as a testimony, and I can't wait to see the ways He moves and works in the time to come."
I will sing, sing, sing, for my God my king, for all else fades away. And I will love, love, love with this heart of mine, for you've been good always.

Journal entry: February 3, 2013

"Knowing about the news I received this week, one would almost expect my prayer to be for healing for my mom. I know that God can heal. I've been memorizing Psalm 103, and there is a verse that says 'who heals all your diseases.' I trust that. I know full well that God can reach down and touch my mom and kill that stupid cancer. I would love that. I would love for my mom to be cancer free and live out her years among us. But Lord, I know myself, and I know my family; and if I were to truly search myself, I would say that is not what my family needs. I don't want mom to have cancer, but I do want to know God deeper and fuller, and if it be through my mom's cancer or more that I come to know God deeper and fuller...then blessed be the name of the Lord."

I had been trying to go on a mission trip to Turkey over spring break, but as soon as I heard that mom had cancer, I canceled those plans, and booked a bus ticket home. There was no question; I needed to spend that week with my mom. Spring break was after her surgery and before she would start chemo, and this would be the healthiest I would see her for a while. The weather was miserable that week in Illinois, and the snow and cold kept us inside. Mom and I cooked together, read books from my childhood, watched movies, and played games. I will always treasure that time I was able to spend with her.

Biopsy—A Waste of Money?

Marcia:

In September of 2012, about four months before I was diagnosed, I had my yearly mammogram at our local hospital as I had done for many years. Afterwards, the radiologist came in and said that she would like to do a biopsy on my *right* breast because she saw what she thought was calcification. She said that this was normal with aging, but she wanted to make sure that it was only calcification. She did the biopsy, and sure enough, that's all it was.

At the time, we felt like it had been a waste of money, since it ate up all of our high deductable of $5,000. Was that biopsy really necessary? In a few months, we would see how God had planned that biopsy for a reason.

Now In November, I felt a lump in my *left* breast. I had experienced many harmless cysts in the past, but this did not feel or act like a cyst at all. Because of the size and shape of this lump and several other symptoms that I had never had before, I began to think that this might be something more serious. I went to Dave and asked if I could get this checked out. Since we had already met our deductible with that "unnecessary" biopsy, we had no reason to wait. Praise God for that! Our met deductible was a blessing, because now we did not hesitate to get this lump checked out. We did not know it at the time, but speed was of the utmost importance since this type of cancer was aggressive and fast growing. God knows what He is doing, doesn't He?

Exodus

Marcia:

I had begun reading through the book of Exodus in my quiet times (spending time alone with God daily by reading the Bible and praying) at the beginning of the year. As soon as I was diagnosed with cancer, I immediately wanted to switch to the New Testament. Sometimes I feel like I can hear the Lord's voice a little easier in the New Testament, so I went before the Lord and said, "Can I go to the New Testament?" I sensed in my heart that He said to keep reading in Exodus. So I kept reading.

I read through the ten plagues, and then again said, "Lord, I'm going through a hard time right now. Can I please go to the New Testament?" Once again I sensed that He was telling me to just keep reading in Exodus. Sigh. So I kept reading.

I read about Moses leading the Israelites out of Egypt, and then WHAM! The Lord spoke powerfully to me. He showed me that just as He had been a pillar of cloud by day to guide the Israelites, so He would be our pillar of guidance. And just as He had been a pillar of fire by night to light their path when it was dark, so He would be our pillar of fire to light our path. And just as He had been their pillar of protection (when the pillar moved from before them to the rear of them to shield them from the approaching Egyptian army), so He would be our pillar of protection. And just as He had provided for all their needs in the wilderness, so He would also provide for all of our needs through this wilderness of cancer.

I was stunned with these four promises. Wow! I had no doubt in my mind that God would do all of these things for us in concrete ways as we went forward. I can hardly talk about this without crying. Throughout this book, you will see how God really did each of these four things in our lives. He is the ultimate promise keeper.

Miracles

Dave:

One day I was driving through a small rural town for work when I passed by a church sign that caught my attention. The sign read, "Every Miracle God Does Begins with a Problem." I thought about that for a while, and realized the truth of this statement.

As I look through Scripture, I see this again and again. From the parting of the Red Sea, to raising Lazarus from the dead, the miracles that God performs solve problems that we cannot solve ourselves. Even the miracle of salvation itself is a result of the problem of sin (and the subsequent consequence of death) that we cannot solve by ourselves.

Many times I find myself wanting to avoid problems in my life. Problems bring pain, stress, and at the very least, inconvenience. They take us out of our comfort zone to a place where we have to depend upon God rather than on ourselves.

We are taught that the American way is to pull ourselves up by our bootstraps, work hard, and solve our own problems. Now, I'm not negating the positive aspects of hard work and planning, but many times God wants us in a position where we need to depend upon Him and not our own self. I came to the conclusion that people do not need to see what Dave can accomplish or solve, but what only God can accomplish in my life. Then He gets the glory and credit that is properly due Him. Marcia's cancer gave me a problem that I could not solve on my own. The many challenges this illness would bring to our lives were taking me into a new place that I had never walked before. I would have to learn to trust and depend upon God with our lives.

When people think of miracles, most of the time they think of only the "big" miracles recorded in the Bible. In addition to the miracles I cited above such as the parting of the Red Sea and the raising of Lazarus from the dead, other big miracles include David killing the giant Goliath, Daniel being protected in the Lion's den, Jesus feeding the 5,000, and Jesus healing the lame and blind. The list can go on and on.

However, I have recently been drawn to the "smaller" miracles that many people forget about that are also recorded in Scripture. For instance, in Deuteronomy 29:5, we read that during the 40 years of wandering in the wilderness by the Israelites, their clothes and sandals did not wear out. Also in 2 Kings 6, we see a man who was a part of Elisha's company of prophets was cutting down trees while building a place to live. While doing this, the axe head fell off the axe and sunk in the Jordan River. The axe head was borrowed and he could not replace it. Elisha threw a stick in the water where it fell in, and the axe head floated to the top and was recovered. Lastly, in Matthew 17:27, we read of Peter finding a four drachma coin in the mouth of the first fish he caught in order to pay both his and Jesus' temple tax.

I could go on with more examples of these "smaller" miracles, but I hope you get the point. God was impressing upon me that these "smaller" miracles show us that God is just as concerned about solving our "smaller" problems in life. He wants to be a part of our lives every day! Just because the problem may seem small to some, it usually is not a small matter to the person that is the recipient of God's work in their life.

Many of the stories we recount in this book may appear to be small miracles. However, they were continual reminders of God's love and presence in our lives as we walked this unfamiliar road called cancer. Whether it was an unexpected financial gift or a well timed encouraging verse of Scripture someone gave us just when we needed it, God's presence many times overwhelmed us to the point of joyful tears.

Promise of Provision

Marcia:

While I was having my quiet time one morning, it dawned on me that I hadn't prayed for financial needs yet. So I prayed, "Lord, I know that there will be bills and expenses that we won't have the money for, so would You provide for all of our needs as they pop up?"

That same day, Dave came home from work and said, "Marcia, you are never going to believe what just happened." Our daughter had two wisdom teeth taken out over Christmas, and now he had stopped by the oral surgeon's office to pay part of the bill. The bill was for $900, and he was going to pay half of it, and ask if he could pay the rest of it when it came in.

After he got there and explained what he wanted to do, the receptionist looked at her computer and said, "Sir, you only owe $50." He asked her how that could be since we don't have dental insurance. She said that she would go and ask someone in the billing department. When she came back, she explained that because of the way her teeth were positioned, they billed it under medical, not dental. Since our deductible was already met, we only owed $50.

I told Dave what I had prayed earlier that day, and we both agreed that God was now promising that He really would provide everything we would need during this cancer adventure. I felt like He was saying that we were covered. We didn't need to worry about a thing.

It was amazing to watch, because all through my tests, treatments and surgeries, there was never a bill or an expense that we couldn't pay. We were a single income family, and my husband didn't have a high paying job. We were helping both of our kids through college as much as we could, and we didn't have much in our savings account. We also had to pay a $5,000 deductible for three years in a row, yet we never needed to have a benefit to raise money to pay for medical expenses. How can we explain this? God was our provider! I still don't know how we did it, except that God miraculously met all of our needs, just like He said He would.

Consecrated Chili

Marcia:

January 2013

After hearing my cancer diagnosis, the next thing our local doctor told us was that we needed to find an oncologist. He gave us one or two names of oncologists in our small rural area, and wished us luck. We looked at each other and kind of scratched our heads and thought—what do we do now? We went home, got on our knees and said, "Lord, we don't know anything about cancer. Show us what to do and where to go."

For the next few days, our lives were turned up-side down. We had the really sad task of calling all of our family and close friends to tell them the news. There is a strong history of cancer in our family which made this task especially difficult. Then we talked with friends who had gone through cancer to see where they had gone for treatment. We still didn't know what to do.

During this time, Lois, a friend from church, fell and broke her shoulder. I organized meals for her and her husband, and I took the first meal. Other people took the next few meals, but I could not find anyone to take the last meal. I made calls, sent emails, and talked to people, but no one could do it. I was really frustrated and developed a bad attitude. I complained to my poor husband saying, "Don't people realize that I'm going through a hard time and need help with this?" Dave calmly reminded me that I had just made a huge pot of chili and suggested that I just take some of that. Great idea! So I made some corn bread, packed up the chili, and off I went.

While I was at her house, Lois said, "Marcia, I just heard that you were diagnosed with breast cancer. Do you remember when I went through breast cancer a few years ago? I highly recommend the cancer center that I went to." Then she gave us a promotional DVD from her cancer center to watch.

Well, I went home and promptly.....ignored the DVD. We were so busy that we just shelved it. A few days later, my husband said let's just stop what we are doing and watch it. When we finished watching it, we looked at each other and thought, is this place for real? It sounds too good to be true. Dave told me to call them the next morning just to "get information." I called the next morning, and I think I talked to an angel for about an hour! This place sounded amazing. When I hung up with her, I immediately called Dave. We both were sensing that this might be where God was directing us to go. Then he called her and talked to her for awhile. She called him back about an hour later and told us:

1) Our insurance was already accepted;
2) They were not in our insurance's network, but would bill us as if they were, saving us thousands of dollars out of our own pockets;
3) They already had five days of consultation appointments and tests lined up for us;
4) They would retrieve all of my test and lab results from our local hospital and doctors for us;
5) They already had five nights of hotels reserved for us *for free*, and every time after that, hotel stays would never cost more than $40 per night;
6) We would eat in their cafeteria *for free* every time we came;
7) We would be reimbursed for gas expenses—from our front door to theirs and back-- *every* time we came, even though it is a three hour trip one way;
8) Even though this cancer center has five locations throughout the country that treat all types of cancer, *this* location also specialized in breast cancer!

UNBELIEVABLE. There was no doubt in our minds now that this was most definitely where God was leading us to. This was a direct answer to our prayer of "show us what to do and where to go." I am convinced that God loves it when His children call out to Him for help, especially when we do it at the beginning.

God had wanted me to take the last meal to Lois so that He could give us one of the biggest blessings of our lives. I see now that it was consecrated chili, used by God. And yes, I feel guilty for complaining about it!

In the Boat

Marcia:

A few months before my diagnosis, Jim Carlson, the interim pastor at our church, preached a sermon on the passage where Jesus calmed the storm (Matthew 8:23-27, Mark 4:35-41). He said that if the disciples had truly known who Jesus was, they would not have been scared at all. They would have been able to enjoy the ride, like an exhilarating roller coaster ride. He said that when he gets to heaven, he wants to jump in with both feet and say, "What a ride!"

After I was diagnosed with cancer, Patty, a friend from church, reminded us of that sermon. As we remembered it, we told ourselves that Jesus was in our boat with us while we traveled through this storm called cancer.

Dave and I were talking about it one day as we sat in our family room at home. Suddenly he jumped up and took a framed picture off our book shelf and said, "Marcia! Look at this!" It was a picture of our family in a river raft, when we had taken a river rafting trip in the Smoky Mountains on a vacation a few years earlier. We have never been ones to buy the souvenir picture that tourist places try to sell you. We are just too cheap! But this one time, Dave had really wanted to buy it.

In this picture, we all had big smiles on our faces as waves splashed around us. In the back of the boat was our guide, and He looked just like how Jesus is pictured in all the paintings! He had long wavy dark hair and a beard. This reaffirmed to us that Jesus was in control, and we could trust Him. This gave us amazing peace as we faced the future. We kept that framed picture in the middle of our living room to continually remind us of this truth.

OUR FAMILY IN THE BOAT WITH "JESUS."

Laughter

Marcia:

I knew that this year would bring hard things, so I asked the Lord to make this a year of laughter. I just didn't want to be beaten down emotionally, struggling to keep my head above water. I still wanted to be able to enjoy life.

Well, the first idea the Lord gave me had to do with wigs. I knew that I would most likely lose my hair with chemo, so Lois, my "chili" friend, took me to see Sue, our local hospital's cancer resource nurse. What a blessing she was! She had rows upon rows of wigs in her office. She closed the blinds and let me try on as many as I wanted.

God had planted a crazy idea in my mind. I tried on a wide variety of wild and crazy wigs; long black hair, bouncy blond curls, short sleek red hair, and even a white "Mrs. Santa Claus" one. We laughed all the way through it, and took pictures of me wearing each one. It was the farthest thing from depressing. What a hoot! Then I went home and posted them all on Facebook!

In the end, I chose a wig that looked very similar to my original color and style. Actually, when I couldn't decide between two wigs, Sue told me to just take them both, and they were all free! Oh Lord--the blessings just kept coming! Now I had one that I wore each day, and one as a backup in case something happened to the other one. Sue also gave me a gift bag from the hospital that was loaded with all kinds of helpful products and encouraging booklets, as well as a gas gift card and a sizeable Walmart gift card. I felt like my cup was already running over with blessings!

I knew the day would come when my hair would begin to fall

out. I had told my husband that when that happened, I wanted him to shave my hair off. I didn't want hair all over the house, as it began to fall out, and I didn't want to begin to feel depressed as it became thinner and thinner.

Then one day I realized it was happening. After my shower, I ran my hand through my hair, and about twenty hairs easily came out. I did it again, and another twenty easily came out. Oh boy, I thought. It's really happening. I called my husband and told him that tonight it was coming off. He said, "Oh, uh, really? Tonight? Are you sure?" The poor guy! I had given him virtually no warning.

That night, before we got started, I told him that I wanted to have fun with it. He got out the electric clippers, and we started trying different hair styles, including a mullet and a mohawk. Dave told me that when he was cutting my hair, it felt like he was a naughty little boy cutting his sister's hair! Then I had a fashion show before him, trying on each wig, several scarves and hats, and voting on which ones we liked the most. It really was a lot of fun.

When I started wearing a wig, I still continued the fun. One time I came to the dinner table and told Dave that I think I need to get my bangs trimmed. I had pulled my wig down to my nose. I also had a wicked dream that someday, when the situation and the timing were just right, I wanted to suddenly pull off my wig in public and freak someone out. It just never happened, and now it's too late. Sigh. God had answered my prayer, though, and gave us laughter during cancer.

Coming Home

Hannah:

I had re-applied for a summer job in Georgia that I had worked at the previous summer, but I knew I was needed at home. Mom told me that if I was offered the job I should take it, and she would be fine with that. I told her absolutely not! I was coming home, and I was going to take care of her. I knew that while being at home I would need to take care of both the house and her. Getting a summer job wouldn't be possible.

As our medical costs were rapidly rising, I didn't know how we were going to be able to pay for my next year of school; However, Mom was more important than school.

I would get home in the middle of her chemo treatments, and I had no idea what to expect. She would call me every few days and tell me how she was, and it was so incredibly hard to listen to her describe how she felt. When she told me about the night that dad shaved her head because her hair was falling out, I bawled on the other side of the phone. I knew that hair was physical and not important, but to me it meant that she would no longer look the same. She would describe her symptoms to me and my heart ached that I wasn't able to be there to take care of her.

Those last eight weeks of school made it very difficult to be fully present in my classes and responsibilities because all I wanted was to be home. At the same time, the closer it came to going home, the more I didn't want to go home. It sounds like a contradiction, but I knew things wouldn't be the same, and that scared me. I knew Mom would look different, and wouldn't be able to do what she normally does when I am home. I dreaded going home to the differences I knew awaited me.

Journal Entry: February 20, 2013

> *"I'm scared. My heart hurts. I don't want to see my mom go through this. I don't want to watch her go through surgery, or watch as they put poison into her body, or watch as her hair falls out, or watch her in pain. It is agony to think about and visualize these things."*

Journal Entry: February 22, 2013

> *"It hurts so bad God. She's having surgery on Monday, and I don't want to talk or skype with them...I'm afraid I'll just start crying. My head hurts from holding in the tears. I can't let them fall...too many people will ask too many questions. I can't let them spill over, not here, not now. God help me. I can't handle this. I'm not strong enough. She's going to look different when I go home in two weeks. I have a feeling I'll be crying myself to sleep. I don't share her attitude, her sense of peace and joy. It doesn't cause me to doubt, God...but the pain is great, and the uncertainty. Am I supposed to go home this summer? Is that why I haven't heard back from my former job? If I go home, will there be a job? If I don't go home, what will happen? Am I needed to be there to cook and clean, to take care of Mom and look after Dad? Or am I supposed to work away from home again this summer, to make money to be able to help pay for college? Which is more important? The answer should be obvious...but I'm scared of going home, of*

watching her go through it. Watching poison spread through her body and cause her pain. The thought causes an ache in my heart and a swelling in my throat. I don't know what to do. Help me Father."

Just for a Season

Marcia:

At the beginning, when I was dealing with heavy things like surgeries and chemotherapy, we would say to ourselves, "It's just for a season," for comfort and encouragement. After a while, I felt like the Lord was telling me to stop saying this, because we really didn't know if it was just for a season. Only He knew the future. If we kept on saying this, and then the cancer returned, it may lead to anger or bitterness or depression if we had convinced ourselves that it is just for a season. We might think that the Lord had let us down. Does God make mistakes? Absolutely not! Who was telling us that it was just for a season in the first place? It was ourselves. We were not getting these reassuring words from the Bible. We had no guarantee whatsoever that I would go through this illness, recover, and be done with it forever. I had to acknowledge that my future was in God's hands, and it was up to me to choose to trust Him no matter what happened in the future.

We tend to worship a problem free life. We crave perfect health. When God hands us a trial by taking away our good health, then our true colors come out. It's so easy to think '*How could you do this to me, God? This is unfair! You let me down! Look at all the problems that have come because of this!*' Basically we're saying '*It's all YOUR fault! Look what YOU did! You messed it all up!*' Did He? Or is He just showing us who really is in control? God is perfect. He is incapable of making mistakes. God wanted us to stop saying "It's just for a season" to keep us from falling into these dangers.

The Body of Christ

Marcia:

From the minute I was diagnosed with cancer, it was amazing to see our spiritual family jump into action. Immediately we began receiving cards, phone calls, emails, and Facebook messages from people who were saying that they were praying for us. Oh how many times Dave and I wept when reading them, especially when they were from people whom we had never met.

We were amazed at how the word spread. People from as far away as Florida, Texas, California, and Alaska were praying for us. How humbling. One couple who lives out of state called us and prayed with us about every two weeks all through the first year. Also, my parents set aside their busy schedules and came for a whole week twice to help us right after two major surgeries.

It made us feel so loved to see our own church do so much for us, too. They brought us meals, gave us gift cards, did our laundry, cleaned our house, went grocery shopping for us, taught Sunday school for Dave, temporarily filled in for Dave on the elder board, and on and on. Sometimes people would call up and ask if they could come over and do whatever I needed help with right then. People will never know how much we really appreciated them.

After my first chemo treatment, I was really knocked down. One woman came over and asked what she could do. I was sitting at the kitchen table in my pajamas staring at a bunch of pill bottles that were swimming in my vision, trying to harness my brain and figure out what to do. I asked her if she could fold all the laundry. I just didn't have the strength to stand and do it. She folded all of our laundry for forty five minutes!

Twice when I was recovering from extensive surgeries, an elderly lady hired someone to clean our house since she was physically unable to do it.

One time after church, a man walked up to us and handed us a card and said that he and his wife wanted to give us a blessing. When we got home, we opened the card and saw that they had given us a check for a sizeable amount.

Another time a woman called us and told us that she was bringing over food for our freezer. She must have been cooking for three days, because she filled half or more of our upright freezer with casseroles, side dishes, and desserts.

One woman in our church told me one Sunday that she was going to shave her head so that I wouldn't be the only one bald. I was deeply touched when she said that. I talked her out of it, though, because I was going to be wearing a wig, and no one would actually see me bald-headed.

One thing really stood out though. Since my husband could only go with me to one of my chemo treatments because he had to work, I prayed that God would raise up people to go with me each time. I knew this was not easy for people to do since it required people to give up one and a half days. The cancer center was three hours away and required an overnight stay in a hotel since I had to get a special shot the next day; but each time, God supplied someone to go with me. Many people really sacrificed to go with me. My sister Carol, who lives two hours away, went with me several times and was also present during many appointments and surgeries. One time a young home schooling mother of five kids went with me. Wow! I will forever be grateful for all the sacrifices they made.

One friend went with me twice! After my chemo treatment one day, she and I went down to the cafeteria to eat dinner. When my friend saw that they were serving fish and stew, she looked at me and smiled and said, "It looks like its pizza night!" We went out, ordered a pizza, and watched a movie in our hotel room. It felt like it was girl's night out! I was able to do this because I usually didn't feel the full effects of chemo until several days later.

I remember another friend who came with me once. We were sitting in my individual chemo bay, and I was hooked up to the IV. We had brought junk food, and were eating and laughing so hard and having such a good time that people would walk by and ask if this was where the party was! God had surrounded us with His amazing family.

One thing that Hannah and I often did throughout that summer was watch re-runs of the show "Extreme Makeover: Home Edition." What a fun thing to do together to watch crazy Ty Pennington lead a huge team of volunteer workers in building beautiful houses for families that were going through extremely hard times. This was a parallel picture of how God had surrounded us with such a wonderful spiritual family while we were going through a hard time.

*Other than family names, I chose not to mention specific names in this chapter

for fear of forgetting someone's name, since so many people helped us.

A Job Loss

Dave:

Another area where God miraculously provided for our family's financial needs happened in our son's life. In May of 2013, Jonathan graduated from Letourneau University with a degree in aeronautical science. He was now a licensed commercial pilot and a certified airplane mechanic (A&P). After his college graduation, he immediately drove up to Alaska to work for a company in Anchorage, and was scheduled to start as soon as he got there. Marcia and I made it to his graduation, and then said our goodbyes as he started his drive from Texas to Alaska. (By the way, even though Marcia was in the middle of her chemo treatments, she was able to go to his graduation and felt great that day in answer to many people's prayers.)

MARCIA WITH JONATHAN AT HIS
COLLEGE GRADUATION, MAY 2013.

After working for this company for one month, he lost his job. The owner of the company really liked him, but realized he needed someone who had more experience than what Jonathan had at this time in his career. What a blow!

He called Marcia at home and told her the news. She burst into tears, tried to encourage him, and then prayed with him. What was God doing? Why had God taken him all the way up to Alaska, only to have this happen? He had just gotten an apartment and was just getting established.

When I heard the news, I began to feel depressed. Would I now need to help Jonathan out financially so he could stay up there and look for another job? Would he need money to return to Illinois? I couldn't afford this right now! I also did not want Marcia to have to worry about this in the middle of her treatments and fight with cancer.

Once again, God proved more than faithful. Jonathan laid low that morning, then updated his resume, contacted his references again, and then hit the streets looking for another job that same afternoon. When Jonathan contacted his references, they all took the time to pray with him over the phone.

God answered! Later that same day, he stopped in at a company that recognized his name. Really? How does that happen? They had an opening and had just been looking through past resumes. They had come across the resume that he had sent before he had graduated. Jonathan gave them his references, and the next day he was hired. Twenty-six hours after losing his job, he had another one!

If that is not enough, this new job had many more benefits and paid him about one-third more than the first one. Wow! When God answers, He really answers. Instead of being a burden and a worry to Marcia and I, it was a source of joy and an opportunity to praise God! He again provided for our family's needs, both financial and emotional.

A Bomb was Dropped

Marcia:

In the fall of 2012, before I was diagnosed with cancer, I left our house one morning to go to a women's Bible study at our church. It was the first lesson of a study on the book of James. I had no idea that a bomb was about to be dropped on my heart that morning.

The leader started out by giving the history behind Jesus' brothers. They all had rejected Jesus until His resurrection, including James, who was the author of the book of James. Then BOOM! God dropped a bomb on my heart when His strong voice of conviction spoke directly to me and said that I was no different than Jesus' brothers, because I have rejected my sister Joyce.

I couldn't wait to go home. I was shell shocked and wanted to process this in private. I knew God was right. I was so very guilty of rejecting my younger sister. She and I had chosen different paths early in life, and our lives had gone in completely opposite directions. I had practically nothing in common with her, and I had virtually ignored her for over twenty years. I only saw her every year around Christmas or Thanksgiving at our extended family gatherings, and although she was nice and friendly, I didn't go out of my way to develop a relationship with her.

When she developed breast cancer before I did, I did nothing. I did not call her or even send her a card. I had sunk so low, and I didn't even know it. How could I have been so blind? How could I have been so uncaring? What had I become? Now God was cracking open my heart and showing me the stinking garbage that was in it.

It took me months to process this. Through this time, I felt the

Holy Spirit urge me to go and visit her and ask her to forgive me for the way I had treated her. I did NOT want to do this. I really, really did NOT want to do this! Me, humble myself before her and admit that I was wrong? Yet that was the truth. How would she react? Would she reject me in return? Would she level her guns at me and let me have it? It would be so awkward.

For the next several months, I put off going to see her. Dave and a friend of mine would ask me once in a while when I was going to see her. Finally, in early December, I climbed on board Amtrak and traveled to Kansas to see her. I was a coward and stayed with my parents at night. I saw her during the day, and amazingly, she treated me like I had been her friend for years. We ate out together, went Christmas shopping together, watched T.V. together, and just chatted.

Finally, when we were sitting alone on her couch talking, I got up my wimpy little courage, took a deep breath and said, "Joyce, I have been a terrible sister to you. I have ignored you for years. Would you forgive me? Can we start over?" She didn't say a word, but she immediately got off the couch and gave me a big hug, and that was it. She never said another word about it. She was so nice and friendly, and treated me like I was a good friend. What a picture of how I should have been to her. I was deeply humbled and ashamed. God was so good to me when I didn't deserve it.

You can guess what happened next. In January, *I* was diagnosed with breast cancer. Now we had something very much in common. Joyce would call me several times a week to see how I was doing as I went through surgeries and started chemo treatments. She was my cheerleader and my coach. God had graciously timed out our illnesses to help us bond together.

In May, my brother Jack had a brilliant idea. He wanted to bring Joyce up to Illinois to visit me in the midst of my chemo treatments. We asked my older sister to join us. He and Joyce drove up from Kansas to our house for the weekend, and my older sister Carol joined us from Chicago. It was possibly the first time that all four of us siblings were together as adults without the extended family.

ALL FOUR OF US SIBLINGS IN BIRTH ORDER L-R,
CAROL, JACK, MARCIA, JOYCE. MAY, 2013.

Joyce was finished with her treatments and her hair was growing out, and I was in the middle of chemo treatments and was wearing a wig. It was a fun time and a precious time. It was a time that I would cherish, because…..it was the last time I saw Joyce.

Right after that weekend, she began to get headaches and backaches. In July, she finally went to see her doctor. The cancer had returned. It had spread to her brain and her bones. Two weeks later, she passed away. We were all stunned that it went that fast.

As we traveled to Kansas for her funeral, I just kept thinking how blessed I was that God gave me a chance to get right with my sister and start a new friendship with her before she died.

IN LOVING MEMORY OF OUR SWEET,
BEAUTIFUL SISTER, JOYCE. 1966-2013.

Aunt Joyce

Hannah:

The year before Mom was diagnosed with cancer, her younger sister Joyce was diagnosed with breast cancer. She was going through treatments of her own when my mom was diagnosed.

This was a very heavy blow to our extended family. Many family members took it very hard because my great-grandmother had died from ovarian cancer, my grandma had died of ovarian cancer, my aunt had breast cancer, and now my mom had breast cancer as well. They were all on my mom's side of the family. My aunt's cancer had gone into remission, but in the middle of the summer (2013), her cancer returned. It had spread to her spine and her brain and she began deteriorating rapidly.

I was counseling at a local Bible camp and began getting letters from my mom telling me that Aunt Joyce didn't have much longer. Hospice had been called, and finally a phone call came telling me that Aunt Joyce had passed away.

That night I was supposed to go to chapel and watch the gospel be presented to 7th and 8th graders, but instead I walked the road around camp and yelled at God. I was so angry at Him for letting Aunt Joyce die. I really vented.

After that night God gave me peace in trusting His will in this situation. It doesn't make sense, and it hurts a lot, but I will trust the Lord. If I knew the mind of God, if I knew His ways and why He does things, then He would not be God. Who is mere man that God would be mindful of him? God loves mere man more than we could possibly imagine, more than we could ever know. He is sovereign. He is good, and all that He does is for our benefit.

The Hardest Time

Dave:

People sometimes ask me what the most difficult time was for me during our journey through Marcia's cancer. By God's grace, we were able to handle this unexpected challenge in our lives better than I would have imagined.

At first, I remember both of us being somewhat emotionally fragile. We cried very easily during this time. However, our tears were not because of fear of the future or due to anger with God for allowing this trial to come into our lives. Each time we broke down and cried, it was tears of joy. Whenever we received an encouraging letter from someone, or were given a timely and meaningful verse of Scripture to hold on to, or found out someone we didn't even personally know was praying for us, we cried. They were tears of joy because they were reminders and expressions of God's loving arms wrapping themselves around us during this uncertain and fragile time in our lives. God was alive, and He was carrying us through this time as we trusted in Him. It was and still is a testimony of God's goodness!

However, it does not mean that it was all easy. The hardest time for me was during the time when Marcia's sister, Joyce, was dying. Marcia had just finished her last chemo treatment two weeks earlier when we made the trip to Kansas for Joyce's funeral.

As we drove there and back, I had a lot of time to think and contemplate these change of events. I know this sounds ridiculous, but all of a sudden I realized that cancer kills! Up to this point, we had been pretty upbeat about this fight against cancer. Yes, Marcia had cancer, but many people get cancer and survive. We felt we were getting excellent care from our cancer center. Treatment was hard, but we could get through it with God's help. Yes, Marcia's sister Joyce had breast cancer too, but she was doing well and appeared to be beating this disease.

When we found out in early July that Joyce's cancer had returned, this challenged our positive way of thinking. When this aggressive cancer took Joyce's life two weeks later, we were shocked. I began to think that this could happen to Marcia as well! Marcia had the exact same kind of aggressive breast cancer that Joyce had. Joyce had received very similar treatment. Cancer had taken the life of Marcia's grandmother, mother, and sister. Cancer seemed to kill everyone who gets it in Marcia's family!

My mind began to race with these thoughts. At this time, I began to prepare myself for the possibility that my wife would not survive. I began to mentally plan her funeral.

This was another test to my faith. Was I willing to trust God with her life no matter what? I don't know why God allowed Joyce to pass away, and Marcia to survive (at least up to this point).

I once heard of a middle aged man, who was dying of cancer, tell his daughter in his last days that, "It is not up to me or you. We don't get to choose if we get an illness or die, but we do get choose how we respond."

I do know that God is infinitely good. God loves us more that we could ever imagine. His love for us was settled on the cross over 2000 years ago. His love is not something that I would question. I would leave Marcia's life in His hands. This was a growing and freeing lesson to learn during Marcia's illness. I don't know what will happen in the future, but I do know that I can trust God for the future.

Time To Grow Up

Hannah:

Summer 2013

For some reason, the concept of Mom without hair was very hard for me. I didn't want to see her bald because I knew that I would probably cry. Mom wanted to ease me into it throughout the summer, but during my first night home, everything changed.

I had just gotten home from school and didn't yet know her routine or how chemo was affecting her on a daily basis. Mom had been having severe abdominal pains from a chemo side affect all day, and they continued to get worse into the evening without letting up. We were in the basement, and Dad had just stepped out of the room when Mom's eyes rolled back in her head and she began convulsing. I stood there shocked, not knowing what to do.

Dad rushed back in and began calling her name and shaking her to wake her back up. Then she threw up. All I could do was stand there. Tears were streaming down my face as I wondered if I needed to call an ambulance.

While Dad was trying to revive her, Mom's wig flew off her head and I saw her bald for the first time. In that moment, I saw my mom not as my mom, but as a person with cancer. It was so incredibly difficult.

That night continued with an emergency room visit until 3 am when she was admitted overnight. The next morning, everything was under control and she was fine, but there was no easing into life with her sick, though. In one night I saw everything in the raw. In that moment I realized that I needed to be an adult this summer.

49

Am I the Mom or the Daughter?

Hannah:

It was a very strange summer for me. When mom was very sick, I took care of her as well as taking care of the house. At twenty years old I was cooking, cleaning, doing laundry, paying bills and running errands as if I were the mom. Then some weeks she would be feeling really good and wanted to do all these things herself. That left me floundering somewhat, not entirely sure what my place was. Some weeks I was the mom, and other weeks I was the daughter.

It was hard switching back and forth like that. I really had to cling to the Lord in the midst of all of this. I was confused and lonely, and didn't know how to handle everything emotionally. It was definitely a growing time both for my family and for myself.

We had many family prayer sessions for financial, physical, and emotional support. The Lord was faithful through it all. He was faithful to give me the strength to make the trip to take my mom to a chemo treatment. He was faithful to give me a lot of time to spend with my dad as we took up jogging together. He was faithful to provide each and every time we needed it. He was faithful.

Unexpected Money

Hannah:

Because I chose to come home to help Mom, I wasn't able to have a summer job. Also, Mom had to give up her part time job, both of which meant that money for next year's school had to come from somewhere else. We covered the situation in prayer, asking God to provide what we needed.

Several years back, the Lord had spoken to my parents and impressed upon their hearts that He wanted them to tithe their income tax refund. They knew that this practice of tithing the income tax refund was not really necessary, as they had already tithed it when it was earned. So to tithe the tax refund was like double tithing. They did it anyway as an act of obedience.

Now that we had a pressing need of $3,000 for next year's tuition, Dad was very tempted to keep the tithed amount of $400 and use it to help pay for my tuition--just this once. He wouldn't keep doing this forever, but just this once. Dad wrestled with this for a while. Use it or tithe it. Use it or tithe it. Eventually Dad said, "No! We are not going to touch it. We are going to tithe it. It's God's money." So they set the $400 aside.

Then I got the idea to petition my school for more financial aid due to Mom's illness. Dad and I filled out piles of required paperwork showing loss of income and increased medical bills. We sent it all off and left it in the Lord's hands. I was hoping for at least $1,000 of extra help. Insider tip: don't limit the Lord's generosity! As the summer progressed I checked my financial aid and discovered that they had added $2,000 to my FAFSA! (Federal student aid)

This was far more than we had expected, and we were thrilled and praised God.

I was jogging with Dad one evening and we discussed that even with that extra money, we were still about $1,000 short of what we needed. He was hopeful that we might be able to come up with what we needed by the time it was due.

When we got back from jogging, I checked my school account again to confirm some numbers. My jaw dropped when I noticed a new scholarship in my account for $1,000. Where did *that* come from? To the penny it was what we needed to pay for the next year of school. When I told my parents, Mom started crying. We were awed by the Lord's faithfulness in providing enough for me to return to the college that I love.

Wait—there's more! A few weeks later I got a phone call out of the blue from the dean of the business department at my school. He told me that my financial aid counselor had contacted him and asked him if there was any way the business department could help me financially. He said that he had found two scholarships for me that when combined amounted to an additional $1,000. I was floored. I was a business administration major, but I had not even taken any business classes yet; only general requirements. I immediately called my parents to tell them the good news! Mom started crying again, of course! Once again we praised God for His faithful provision.

Do you see what happened? Because my dad was obedient and gave up $400, God blessed us with $4,000. And not only did the Lord provide for my next year of college, but He provided $1,000 above and beyond what we initially needed. Now we had extra that we could put aside for the next semester.

I did not have a paying job that summer because my job was caring for my mom and running the house as best I could. So what did the Lord do? He provided us with $4,000 for school which is much more than I could have made at a summer job, and it was all tax free and went straight toward my tuition. He allowed me to stay at home where I was needed, and He allowed me to be able to return to school. God didn't just provide for our family as a whole, but He provided for me personally to be able to continue my education at the school that I loved.

HANNAH GRADUATING FROM
MISSISSIPPI COLLEGE, MAY 2016.

Learning to Live by Faith

Dave:

I suppose that I am a typical man, husband and father. I want to provide for my family, protect them, and fix the problems that we face; but now I didn't know if I could provide for the financial challenges that our family would face. I could not protect my wife from this terrible disease that had attacked her body, and I could not imagine all the problems and decisions that we'd face. I did not have a clue as to how to fix them.

I have always been a planner. I anticipate our needs, and then plan accordingly. This is one of the ways in which I managed my anxiety. If I properly planned, then I did not have to worry about the future. While this can be a good quality, its weakness is struggling to live by faith. This is an area that I needed to grow in. Was I willing to trust God with my wife's health, life, and future?

Our daughter Hannah and I had a conversation about this about a year before. Hannah is very much like me in personality and planning tendencies. While she could relate to me in this area, she also saw my weak spot and challenged me to learn to trust in the LORD--not just with words (which of course is easy), but in action. When the doctor told us it was cancer, I knew right away that God was giving me an opportunity to grow in this area.

Later that year, Marcia and I were studying the book *Experiencing God* (revised and expanded edition) by Henry and Richard Blackaby, in our Sunday school class. One day when I was reading this book, a paragraph jumped out at me. It said, "Christians (as well as everyone else) have a natural tendency to try building a life in which faith is unnecessary. We establish a comfort zone where everything is in our control, but this is not pleasing to God. God will allow things into our lives that drive us to utter dependence upon Him. Then we see His power and His glory. " (p. 210.) Wow! That just described my life! Now God was allowing cancer into our lives to drive me to utter dependence upon Him. I needed this!

By God's grace and patience, my faith has improved. God was faithful in every area of our lives over the next few years. And do you know what? It was exciting to see! I got a front row seat to watch God at work! My faith grew as I depended on God to do what I could not.

One area that was particularly challenging for me was to learn to trust Him for our financial needs. As you have read from Marcia and Hannah, God provided miraculously for our financial needs in many different ways. Hannah shared how God provided the funds she needed to return to school in the fall of 2013. For me, the test had been to give to God first (tithe our income tax refund as He had directed me to), and trust Him with our future needs. It was a stretching act of faith.

As an addendum to this story, God challenged me again in this area two years later. It was the spring/summer (2015) before Hannah's senior year of college. We had depleted our funds for college for that spring semester. As a matter of fact, we were in the hole. (I borrowed from Peter to pay Paul in our budget.) We were, however, blessed to have received another sizeable income tax refund. Remembering our past, I again (without question this time) tithed our income tax refund by giving 10% to the Lord's work. This still left a good portion to start the funding of Hannah's education for the next year.

In May, Marcia and I had the unique privilege to meet and get to know a pastor and his wife from Nepal who were visiting our church. This was a man who was obedient to God's call in his life to be a pastor and a leader of many churches that he planted, and was also obedient to house many orphans in his own home. All of this was done while being very poor and persecuted.

They also had a daughter named Hannah who was the exact same age as our daughter Hannah. Their daughter Hannah had been accepted to a Bible school in the Netherlands with a full scholarship, but they did not have the financial means to get her there. They needed $1,350 for her airfare.

That evening God impressed on my heart that we should give money to their Hannah. We were to take some of the money we had saved for our Hannah's education, and give it to them for their Hannah's education. What?! We need this money! I've already given my tithe!

I woke up in the middle of the night and could not sleep as I wrestled with this new instruction from the Lord. Finally, I gave in. I loudly sighed and said out loud, "OK!" I knew the money was not mine. It was God's. I would give it to them for their Hannah's education, and trust God for the money for our Hannah's education.

In the morning, Marcia asked me what I said in the middle of the night. Oh great! She heard that? Now God was making sure I went through with it!

God proved faithful once again. Later I acquired a new account for work that brought in much more money than I would have planned on. I had to work many long hours, but God more than replaced the money we needed to send Hannah back to school in the fall.

God was not done though. We were unaware of something else. That spring, Hannah, along with Marcia, had attended an honors banquet at her college. While at the banquet, she and Marcia had been seated next to the donor of one of the scholarships that Hannah had graciously received during her time at Mississippi College. They had a chance to thank him again, this time in person. However, unbeknownst to them, after the banquet this gentleman approached the dean of Hannah's department and gave him a $1,000 check to be put towards Hannah's education! For some unknown reason, we were not made aware of this, and it wasn't applied to her school account until September. If we had known in the spring about this gift, our gift to the pastor in Nepal would not have been a gift of faith at all. God again gets all the glory.

As of the writing of this book, Hannah has now graduated from Mississippi College. With God's provision, she graduated debt free! When Marcia was diagnosed with cancer in 2013, I would *never ever* have imagined that with all of our medical bills, Hannah would graduate debt free. This brings to mind the verse of Ephesians 3:20 "Now to Him who is able to do immeasurably more than all we ask or think..." (NIV) God continues to build my faith.

An Unexpected Gift

Hannah:

Journal Entry October 23, 2013

"It's been a while since I last wrote, perhaps because I didn't know what to write about, or perhaps because I didn't want to face things by writing them. Whatever the reason, what better way to break that than by praising Jesus for his goodness? I have been missing my parents so much this semester, more than usual. Mom is having surgery tomorrow, and I so wish I could be home to take care of her as she recovers. I have been stressing a lot about getting home for Christmas. With a really late finals schedule, rides and tickets home are scarce and expensive. I came back to my room after a meeting last night to find an envelope slid under my door. It said "For Hannah, here's your ticket home." Inside was $177 in cash. I was blown away. I immediately started crying. That someone would care enough and follow the Lord's leading like that meant so much. I mean, that is so much money! I don't know anyone who has any money to spare, let alone that much. The Lord is so faithful to provide. Who am I to doubt him? He has never failed me. Even when I am unfaithful, He remains faithful and pours out blessings I don't deserve. I will praise his name for He is good!"

Blessed While Waiting

Dave:

In October of 2013, Marcia was scheduled for a pretty big six hour surgery. She had already had two previous operations. Now came the third surgery, to proactively help reduce her risk for future cancer recurrence (since she tested positive for the defective breast cancer gene BRCA1), and to begin the first step of breast reconstruction. This surgery would have three different parts and involve three different surgeons.

As a result of the length and complexity of the surgical coordination, Marcia was worried that I would have to endure a long boring day of waiting. Because of the distance of our cancer center from our home, it would not be easy for friends or relatives to come and be with me during the surgery.

As it turned out, Marcia needn't have worried. God had my day well planned out. It began with the surgery prep. When the plastic surgeon came in to examine Marcia, I closed the privacy curtain. However, after he left, I forgot to open the curtain back up. Therefore, the nursing staff who had not seen the doctor leave, thought he was still examining Marcia. The surgery was supposed to start at 7:30. They finally came in at 7:55 and realized the mistake. As a result, the surgery started half an hour late.

Meanwhile, I went to the cafeteria to eat breakfast. When I was almost done, I was approached by one of the chaplains on staff at the cancer center and was asked if I wanted to join a group of men for breakfast in the private dining room. I most certainly did! For the next hour or more, I enjoyed the company of other men who either had cancer or were caregivers for someone in their lives who had cancer. I heard men testify of how God was working in their lives and doing miracles that were transforming the way they lived. I was also given the opportunity to share my testimony of how God was working in our lives! It was a tremendous blessing to be a part of this fellowship of men who encouraged each other with God's Word and His works in their lives.

I also connected with one man in particular from Ohio that was there as a caregiver for his wife. I saw him several times over the next two days and was blessed to be able to pray with him and encourage him. I also got to meet his wife and encourage her as well. None of this would have happened if Marcia's surgery would not have been delayed. I would have eaten breakfast earlier and not had the opportunity to be involved in this breakfast and meet these men.

As the day progressed, I saw and met with this chaplain several times. I also saw my new friend from Ohio several times.

I also ran into a woman whom Marcia and I had met back in February who had gone through breast cancer and had faced many of the same things Marcia was going through. She was a real encouragement to me that day. Later my parents showed up to offer their support. I also spoke with each surgeon during and after their parts of the surgery.

The day just flew by! God not only provided things for me to do, but He provided plenty of spiritual encouragement and support from many people. Even though Marcia was in surgery for over six hours that day, I was well taken care of and provided for. She cruised through the surgery with flying colors.

I've Got Reason to Worry, Don't I?

Marcia:

From the beginning of my cancer diagnosis, God gave me an amazing blanket of peace. I truly was not worried about anything. It was incredible! I didn't lay awake at night with thoughts like *did they get it all? What if it comes back? Will our daughter get breast cancer?* I realized that I had more reason to worry than most people because:

1) I had been diagnosed with an aggressive fast growing type of cancer. I had been told that if it came back, it would be before five years, and most likely in the first year.

2) My sister had the same kind of cancer and passed away from it, which convinced us that this cancer was deadly.

3) I tested positive for the breast cancer gene, which meant that my chances of cancer returning are really high.

4) Our daughter tested positive for the breast cancer gene, which means her chances of getting cancer are really high.

Amazingly, God had given me a special gift of peace. I began to see how priceless it was. I was not hounded constantly with worries that I could do nothing about.... *until my next surgery.*

I had already undergone a six hour surgery, and now I was scheduled to have a complicated ten hour breast reconstruction surgery. Whoa! That is a long time to be under anesthesia! Anesthesia is always risky, where you are hovering just above death; and ten hours of anesthesia? What if I didn't wake up? I had such peace about dying, because I knew I would wake up in heaven, but what about those left behind? I just couldn't bear the thought of the terrible grief and pain my husband and family would go through, and all of my daily work that my husband would have to do while working full time if I was gone. Now worry was nipping at my heels like a dog. Why did I have peace about the six hour surgery, but not about this ten hour surgery?

Then one day I sensed that the Lord was telling me that it was time to deal with this worry. I knew He was right. I sat down alone with the Lord and told Him everything that I was worried about. Then I realized that I needed to let God handle it, no matter how it turned out. I discovered that it really was a trust issue. I needed to trust Him with it all. Could I trust Him to take care of my husband and family if I died? Then I said the words, "Yes Lord, I trust You." Then my peace was restored. I no longer dreaded this lengthy surgery. If I was offered any gift in the whole world, I would choose peace. Peace. Is. Awesome.

Fight for Me!

Marcia:

A few days before the big ten hour reconstruction surgery, I asked the Lord for a theme verse for the surgery. He immediately gave me Exodus 14:14 "The LORD will fight for you; you need only to be still." (NIV) The context is this: Moses had led the Israelites out of Egypt. Now they were trapped between the Red Sea and the approaching Egyptian army. They were beginning to panic. Moses wisely told them to keep still while the Lord fought for them. Now God was telling me to be still and watch Him fight for me during this surgery.

Three things happened to me following my surgery in which I called out to the Lord to fight for me.

1) After the surgery while in ICU, I started to feel nauseated. The thought of throwing up when I had three fresh incisions in my chest and abdomen really scared me. I was so weak and could barely move. I asked the Lord to fight for me. He answered by having the nurses give me an anti-nausea drug. That really helped.

2) However, this drug wore off about five hours later and could not be given again for another three hours. I was then given an additional different anti-nausea drug. Although this drug also took away the nausea, it brought a frightening side affect. It felt like there was an elephant sitting on top of my chest, making it difficult to breath. I thought that if I fell asleep, I would stop breathing. Each breath felt labored and

shallow, which was so scary. Once again, I called out to the Lord to fight for me. He did, and eventually this heaviness left.

3) Then, at the doctor's request, we spent the weekend in a nearby hotel so that he could see me again on Monday before I went home. Well, over the weekend, I had a horrible bout with constipation. My bowels hadn't moved in almost a week, and now I was in agony with severe cramping. Once again I called out to the Lord to fight for me. My sweet and dedicated husband went out at 11 p.m. and got what I needed. That night we bonded in new and unforgettable ways as he lived out his vows of "for better or for worse!" In the morning, I was cleaned out and felt like a new woman, although exhausted.

God really did fight for me while I was so helpless. He gets *all* the praise and glory!

Interesting side story: While we were preparing to leave home for this surgery, we looked at the calendar and realized that I had my first breast removed on February 23rd, 2013, and now I would have new breasts added with this reconstruction surgery on February 23rd, 2014, *exactly* one year later to the day.

Also, right before we left the house to drive to the cancer center for this surgery, I pulled a verse out of a flower pot on our kitchen counter that holds a hundred or so Bible verses. I read it to Dave, and we both cracked up laughing.

Zechariah 9:12b (NLT)

> "I promise this very day that I will repay two blessings for each of your troubles."

God has a sense of humor, doesn't He?!

Open Your Mouth

Marcia:

In January 2014, Randy Sizemore, our new pastor, had begun preaching through the book of Joshua. Joshua was about to lead the children of Israel into a new land, the land God had promised them. I sensed that the Lord was saying to me that I was just about to enter a new land as well. I was leaving the wilderness of cancer, and was about to enter the land after cancer.

In the first chapter of Joshua, Joshua is told to be strong and courageous three times from God, and once from the people. Pastor Randy said that God was taking Joshua, who had been Moses' assistant, and was telling him to suit up—it's time to get in the game. I said, "Lord, are you trying to tell me something?" I felt that He was telling me to "suit up" too.

Then as Joshua was giving instructions to the people, he told them that the ark of the covenant (the presence of God) would go before them. I felt like God was also telling me that He would go before me. I was to keep Him in my sights and follow Him.

Then a verse stood out from chapter one that really scared me. Ch. 1:14 said "....you shall cross before your brothers in battle array...."(NASB) This is repeated again in 4:12 "...crossed over in battle array..." (NASB) I asked Dave, "Does this mean that we will now be facing battles? Will we be attacked?" He wisely said that the Israelites were not on the defensive, but were on the offensive. They were seeking out their enemies and were attacking *them*. In all but one instance (because of the sin of one man), the Lord gave them victory.

At Dave's request, I had been writing down all the amazing things that God had done for us in a journal that I had entitled *"Book of Miracles."* Dave told me that we need to be strong and courageous and tell people these things to show them God's power in our lives. I am an introvert by nature, and would rather listen to others than do the talking. Now God is telling me to speak up? Strength and courage needed, Lord! The Lord impressed upon me that I would be going into enemy territory, but He would give me victory. Now I'm shaking in my boots! But the words of chapter one gave me peace: 1:5 "….I will be with you; I will not fail you or forsake you" (NASB), and 1:6 "Be strong and courageous" (NASB).

When Pastor Randy preached on Joshua chapter 3, another verse stood out to me. Joshua 3:5 says, "Then Joshua said to the people, consecrate yourselves, for tomorrow the Lord will do wonders among you." (NASB) I didn't know exactly what consecrate meant, so I asked Pastor Randy what it meant. Some versions say consecrate, and some say sanctify. They both mean about the same thing; to purify yourself and separate yourself from sin. I asked the Lord to show me sin in my heart that I needed to clean out. Right away He pointed out a relationship that I had damaged years ago that I needed to repair. Immediately I burst into tears. This would be so hard, yet I needed to do it. It is now a work in progress.

Stones Underwater

As I was reading Joshua chapter 4, I saw that God told the Israelites to do something tangible to help them remember His powerful works in their lives. God told the Israelites to take twelve large stones from the middle of the Jordan River to the other side of the river and make a memorial with them. Then throughout the years when their children asked what that pile of stones was there for, they could tell them about the power of God and all the wonderful miracles He did for them.

Then in vs. 9, it says that Joshua made another pile of large stones in the middle of the river. This made me insanely curious! Why did he build a memorial pile of stones in the middle of the river? When the water returned, you would not have been able to see it. I searched through commentaries and on the internet, and asked the Lord to show me why Joshua did this.

Finally I found an answer. I don't know if this was his real reason or not, but it meant a lot to me. The water was high at the flood stage then when God parted the river, but what would they see when the water was low? They would see a reminder of the power of God. Someday, there will be a drought, maybe in my own spiritual life, or maybe as the end times come nearer and sin is spiraling out of control. That is when we will see the pile of stones and remember that we really do serve a powerful God who is still in control and who is still active in our lives. So I kept writing in my "book of miracles," and am now writing for everyone to read. We will need these reminders of God's power in times of drought.

Not Alone

Then I read Joshua 5:13-15 which says, "Now it came about when Joshua was by Jericho, that he lifted up his eyes and looked, and behold, a man was standing opposite him with his sword drawn in his hand. Joshua went to him and said to him, "Are you for us or for our adversaries?" He said, "No; rather I indeed come now as captain of the host of the LORD." And Joshua fell on his face to the earth, and bowed down, and said to him, "What has my lord to say to his servant?" The captain of the LORD's host said to Joshua, "Remove your sandals from your feet, for the place where you are standing is holy." And Joshua did so."(NASB)

This was fascinating to me. I perceived that the Lord was teaching me two things through this. 1) The angel was telling Joshua that there was an army of angels (the "host of the Lord") that would also be fighting the battle; and 2) Joshua was in the presence of the Lord (the place where you are standing is holy).

I realized now that I would not be going into the world alone, but an army of angels would be fighting with me, and I would be in the presence of the Lord when I go out. This was so reassuring.

A Nurse in the Night

Marcia:

The first time I felt like the Lord loosened my tongue was with one person. After I had my ten hour breast reconstruction surgery, I was in ICU for a few days afterwards.

One night, in the middle of the night, a nurse named Abbie came in to take my vital signs and do a few other things. She was constantly working. She had the energy of a bumble bee and was just amazing! I was wide awake, so I told Abbie that I really appreciated all the work she did, and that she was a really good hard worker. She thanked me and then left. About two minutes later, she came back in and thanked me again for saying that, because she said they just don't hear things like that very often.

We struck up a conversation, and I began to tell her some of the amazing things that the Lord had done over the past year in our lives. After awhile, she pulled up a chair and sat down. Then she pulled out a Kleenex and started dabbing her eyes. When I was finished, she said that I will never know how much that meant to her. She said that she really needed to hear all that I said. We started a friendship that continued after I was discharged. God was using her to get me started.

Nicole

Marcia:

Another person that the Lord put in my path to help me reach out to others was a young woman named Nicole. One day when I was at my cancer center sitting in a waiting room, I noticed a young woman nearby who seemed emotionally distraught. I overheard her say to a man next to her something about losing her hair. There was a middle aged man and woman on the other side of her who were trying to comfort her. I felt prompted to speak up, so I tried to say some encouraging words. Then she was called out for her appointment. A little while later, I was called out for my appointment too.

While I was passing in front of them, the older man thanked me for encouraging her. He said that her name was Nicole and she was their daughter, and was here with her fiancé. She was only 28 years old, and had just been diagnosed with breast cancer. Their wedding was just a few months away. I said that when I got back from my appointment, if they were still here, I would love to talk with them if they were interested.

After my appointment, I met up with them in the hallway. We seemed to bond immediately, and before we parted ways, Nicole seemed calmer. We exchanged contact information, and she gave me a big hug.

Soon after that, Nicole and I became friends on Facebook. I shared my experience with her and did my best to cheer her on. Then I asked all of my Facebook friends to pray for her, especially with her wedding coming up. So many people responded that they were praying for her.

Another time when I was at my cancer center for a check-up, I suddenly realized that this was the same day that Nicole was scheduled to have her first chemo treatment. I texted her and asked if she wanted me to drop in and see her during her treatment before I started for home. She said yes, but her treatment didn't start for a couple of hours. My appointment was already over. What would I do until then?

Then God gave me an idea to go to Walmart and put together a chemo care package for her. I drove to Walmart and said, "Lord, I don't know what to put into a chemo care package. Show me what to get." I picked out a large pink gift bag, and randomly walked through the aisles. I filled it with whatever stood out to me. I really didn't know what I was doing. I hadn't talked to my husband about this, and wondered if all of this would fit into our budget, but I sensed the Lord was saying don't worry about it.

When I found Nicole in her chemo bay, her chemo infusion had already started and she was sobbing. My heart broke for her. Her mom and dad and fiancé were there, and were doing whatever they could to help her. I gave her the gift bag, and immediately they pulled out a really soft blanket that I had picked out. She was shivering, so they wrapped it around her. I asked her if I could pray for her, and she said yes. After I prayed, she gave me a big hug and thanked me for coming. She told me later that when I prayed for her, a sense of peace came over her, and pain that she had been feeling vanished.

Later, I received a really sweet thank you note from her. She said that everything in the gift bag was perfect, and she had used it all. She asked how I knew what the perfect things were to put in this package? Haha. I didn't know, but God did. Everything was exactly what she needed. She told me later that the blanket was her favorite, and she was constantly wrapped in it at home.

Awhile later, I asked God what I should do next for Nicole. Her wedding was coming up soon, and Dave and I had been invited. We accepted and were looking forward to attending.

Then, about a week before the wedding, God planted another idea in my mind. I asked our church secretary to send out a church-wide email asking people to pray for Nicole that week and the day of her wedding, and to send her a note telling her that they were praying for her. I just couldn't imagine getting married while undergoing chemo treatments, so I wanted to get the body of Christ to lift her up in prayer and ask God to give her what she needed for her big day.

The day of the wedding arrived, and Nicole was a stunningly beautiful bride, even with a wig. The music started, and then a few extra songs were played. Then she walked down the aisle.

Later Nicole explained to me that those "extra" songs were added because she had suddenly developed urgent bathroom issues. They had to quickly undo her dress, and she barely made it to the bathroom in time. She did make it down the aisle though, and did very well the rest of the evening. Can you imagine if those bathroom issues had kicked in while she was at the altar? (Nicole gave me permission to share all of this.)

On her wedding day, God had given her what she needed and had timed out the crisis perfectly. He had answered all of our prayers for her. When we went through the receiving line, Nicole hugged me tightly and profusely thanked me and everyone in our church who had prayed and sent so many notes to her. God is so good, isn't He?

Being a Caregiver

Dave:

What does it mean to be a caregiver? This was something I needed to learn and depend upon God for. First, we faced the unknown, because we knew next to nothing about cancer treatment or care. Once we found out all of what we'd be going through, the task became more defined. I sensed early on that Marcia was going to need me in ways that she never had before. Was I up to the task? What changes needed to be made in my life so that I could be the caregiver Marcia would need?

I decided to seek out council from some older men that had traveled this path before. I spoke with my dad and a man in our church whose wife had been battling breast cancer for the past few years. Through these conversations, it became clear that I needed to free up my time to focus on Marcia. She was now the priority. Ministry in the church, personal interests, hobbies, and the like would have go. If I was going to live out my marriage vows, adjustments needed to be made.

I saw this as an opportunity to serve my wife. What a joy and privilege it was. I stepped down from most of my responsibilities as an elder in our church, teaching Sunday school, and leading our small group Bible study. In each case, God provided others to step up and take on these responsibilities for me. I did still have to work full time. We needed the money and insurance benefits, so unfortunately I was not able to go to all of Marcia's appointments and treatments. However, God worked it out so that other friends and relatives were able to help fill in the gaps. Thankfully, I was able to be there at every one of Marcia's major surgeries and much of her other care and consultations.

One night, as we were staying in a hotel near the hospital recovering from Marcia's ten hour surgery, she became sick. I ended up having to clean up the bathroom floor from a pretty bad accident. If I remember right, I had Kleenex stuffed up my nose so that I would not throw up over the smell. I looked ridiculous with Kleenex hanging out of my nose, but we now laugh about it as a time when we bonded in a new way as never before.

I don't regret my decision to care for and make Marcia my priority in the least. That year of fighting cancer gave Marcia and I more time together than we'd had in a long, long time. God used that time to draw us closer together as a couple and closer to Him.

Breast Cancer Gene

Hannah:

During the time that my mom and aunt were sick at the same time, we discovered that they both had the same mutated breast cancer gene that had caused their cancer. It is called BRCA1, and yes, this is the same gene that the actress Angelina Jolie has as well. Although there is no way that my grandmother could now be tested to see if she had the gene as well, we assume that she did, as it is a hereditary mutation.

My grandmother died when she was 45, my aunt died when she was 46, and my mom was diagnosed when she was 48. After my aunt passed away, we began to see the reality of this very aggressive type of cancer, and how deadly it can be.

Because it is a hereditary gene mutation that causes both breast and ovarian cancer, it was logical to assume that I could have inherited this mutated gene as well. We discussed what that could mean for me.

Through counseling from both my parents and advice from a genetic counselor at my mom's cancer center, I made the decision to be tested to see if I had the mutated gene as well. My parents left this decision up to me. I was twenty years old, and finding out if I tested positive or negative was a decision they allowed me to make.

It wasn't very difficult for me to make this decision because I knew that the knowledge could only help me. Some people think that it is not right for them to know things like this, and that it should all be left in God's hands. While I agree to an extent, I believe that God gives us knowledge and tools to help us make decisions wisely. There are screenings and preventative procedures available that can greatly reduce the risk of breast and ovarian cancer. I wanted to know if I would need them in the future.

I wanted to know if I had the mutated gene, but I was scared that it might be positive. I wasn't afraid of dying because of the hope I have in Christ and the knowledge that I will spend eternity in heaven, but after watching my mom go through cancer, I knew that I did not want to go through that myself.

I had a lot of fear resurface during the next month before the test, but it was a perfect opportunity to see how much I was truly willing to trust the Lord. I knew that if I tested positive, then I would have between a 50% - 87% chance of getting breast cancer at some point in my life. Seeing the pattern in my family, I am most likely to be diagnosed sometime in my 40's, unless I take preventative measures.

Journal Entry August 19, 2013

> *"Last night Mom, Dad and I went to church to hear missionaries from Honduras talk about their previous year of ministry in Honduras. One thing they said that hit me was that when you go through hard times, give praise to Jesus because it is completely contrary to the world, and it foils the enemy. This struck my heart as I thought to myself that my fear of this test has no place in my life. Romans 8:28 says, "And we know that for those who love God, all things work together for good, for those who are called according to his purpose." (ESV) I may think I know what is good for me, but only God sees all and knows all; and if I have the promise of God that all things will work together for good, then fear of the future, of the unknown has no place in my life. From now on, I don't want to live in a "spirit of fear, but in power, love and self control." 2 Timothy 1:7 (ESV) I don't want to live in fear of*

my mom's cancer returning or in fear of her dying, or in fear of my test being positive. God alone knows what is truly good for me, and whatever he has me go through in this life is another opportunity to trust him and praise him, no matter how painful. God, if you choose to take my mother, I will still praise you for you are good. If my test is positive for the BRCA1 gene, I will still praise you for you are good. "I have said these things to you, that in me you may have peace. In the world you will have tribulation (trial, suffering, something that causes great suffering), but take heart; I have overcome (overpower, succeed in facing up to a problem or difficulty, defeat, overwhelm, subdue) the world." John 16:33 (ESV-minus the words in parenthesis)

During the time before the test, one scripture stood out to me, and I held onto it as my own personal mantra: *"For the righteous will never be moved; he will be remembered forever. He is not afraid of bad news; his heart is firm, trusting in the Lord. His heart is steady; he will not be afraid."Psalm 112:6-8a (ESV)*

This passage of scripture gave me a lot of comfort and peace, and made me realize that no matter what outcome the test gave me, there was nothing to fear in it. Putting my trust in the Lord for this result meant that I believe that God has my best interest in mind, and that whatever happens in my life, good or bad, all glory will go to God. I firmly believe that God is sovereign and loves without condition, and that knowledge gives me a peace that gets me through every day.

I was tested for the mutated gene in August, and was asked to come back in September to get my result. However, I was just about to go back to school twelve hours away and knew that coming back in September was not possible. The hospital has a policy against sending test results like this in the mail, so they were going to make me wait and come in December when I was home over Christmas break. I didn't think I could wait that long to find out. Three months more of wondering did not appeal to me. Thankfully the genetic counselor and the doctor were willing to work with me and agreed to call me with the news in September as long as I promised to come in for a follow-up visit in December.

It was a simple blood test, and the nurse, genetic counselor, and doctor were all very professional and courteous to me. They treated me like an adult and respected my desire to have this test done. After the test was done, I went home, then back to school and placed the result in God's hands.

Test Results

Hannah:

Journal Entry September 20, 2013

"*I received a phone call on Wednesday from the genetic counselor from the cancer center. They told me that I tested positive for the BRCA1 gene mutation. I wasn't very surprised. My gut feeling was that I was positive. Though it wasn't a shock, it was no less painful to hear. I know I did not receive a cancer diagnosis, or a death sentence, but I feel as though I am guaranteed to get breast cancer in my 40's unless I take major preventative measures. That's a freaking hard reality to deal with. I didn't cry. I still haven't. I've taken it much more calmly than I expected to, but I feel like I'm waiting for it to hit, and then there will be ugly crying.*

A dear friend was there for me, to hold my hand and ask me what I needed. I told Mom the news, and afterwards she said that she bawled and bawled for me. Dad was more pragmatic and that night transferred a gift of money into my checking account. He said he had wanted to send me flowers, but thought I would rather spend the money on what I liked. He knows me so well."

Journal Entry September 25, 2013

"God is ever faithful, l and I should not be surprised by this. He has been with me, holding me, singing over me. He has given me the strength to process, cope well with, and give glory to the One who alone knows why all this is happening.

He brought me the prayer and sweet support of a brother on campus whose encouragement and bold prayer meant more to me than he knows. He was with me in my tests that I felt so unprepared for, and ended up doing well in. He is with me as I continue to make new friends and strengthen current friendships. He uses friends to prompt me to buy books that speak to my soul. He orchestrated my small group of four that is so intimate, sweet, and encouraging. He prompts people to message me on Facebook that encourage and uplift me.

Why do we fear bad news? God sustains. We say that God won't give us more than we can handle. I disagree. I believe he is always giving us more than we can handle, because then our only choice is to cling to Jesus and His promises. Through that our lives give glory to God."

Mission Trip to Honduras

Hannah:

Journal Entry March 19, 2014

"I'll admit, it was difficult for me to have *Debbie
on the trip. It was difficult to watch her, diagnosed in
August, stage 4, eight rounds of chemo. She worked
the whole time, had no major side effects, and came
on this trip just after finishing chemo. She walked
around without a wig like it was no big deal. She
worked harder than almost any of us. I was astounded
by her stamina.

Don't get me wrong, I admire her so much for coming
on this trip in her condition, but I just couldn't help
comparing her to my mom. By all standards, my mom's
cancer was better than Debbie's, but it had hit mom
so much harder. Granted, Mom is about twenty years
older than Debbie, and I know that makes a huge
difference in how their bodies will react, but it's still
hard to see. I'm happy for Debbie, and I'm glad her
cancer has been so easy for her, but for some reason it
escalated my pain for my mom.

Debbie gave her testimony on Friday, and she said
something so profound: "If I live, I will live for God,

and if I die, I will live with God." I had been fighting tears since she started talking about her cancer, but when she said that, I lost it. I left the capilla and went outside and ugly cried about Mom and me and cancer and BRCA1 for the first time ever. Why it took so long to catch up with my emotions I don't know. It was hard, but good. I'm glad Debbie was on the trip. It put things into perspective. There were things I said that she couldn't relate to, but she definitely humbled me by being on this trip."

*Debbie—not her real name.

It may seem like there were a lot of journal entries in my part of telling this story, but I included them because they consist of my uncensored thoughts, thoughts I wanted to share with everyone who reads this. You see, I'm not perfect, and I still struggle with thoughts of worry and fear, but ultimately my hope and peace rest in Christ Jesus. That brings me such great joy.

This season of my mom having cancer, and getting my own test results for a cancer gene has been incredibly hard, but one that I have been privileged to go through. This might sound strange or backwards, but I do not wish that this season of cancer had not happened. In fact, I thank God for it because I saw Him do things above and beyond all that I could have asked or imagined Him to do. He was my comforter, my provider, my Savior, my friend. When I was overcome with fear about the future and the unknown, God provided me with clarity and peace.

At the writing of this book, I am twenty-two years old, and have no idea what the future holds for my health and my mom's health; but I can tell you this: I no longer fear the future or what news may come, because my hope rests in the one who knows all things, and who loves me unconditionally.

Another Special Gift

Marcia:

One November evening after all of my treatments had ended, my husband and I were invited to dinner at our next door neighbor's house. We had known Andy and Audrey for a number of years and were good friends with them.

After dinner they asked if we were still planning on going to visit our son Jonathan who lived in Alaska. We had been wanting to visit him, and had never been to Alaska. This might be our only chance to see Alaska while he still lived there.

I replied that I had recently looked into flight costs, but didn't know if we could do it because the airfare was extremely expensive. Andy and Audrey got a funny look on their faces and told us they wanted to give us an early Christmas card. We opened it and saw that they were giving us 50,000 frequent flyer miles so that we could go to Alaska and see Jonathan. I started crying. How extremely generous! Wow! This was a dream come true! They worked with us and helped us book the tickets using their frequent flyer miles.

We flew to Alaska in early July. The mountains were unbelievably gorgeous! Jonathan, who is a pilot in Anchorage, took us on a stunning sight-seeing flight over mountains and glaciers. He also took us hiking *on* a glacier. That was so cool!! We hiked for three hours. I didn't want to stop. I had prayed so much that God would give me energy and stamina for this trip, and He really did. Who would have thought that my weakened body was up to that much hiking? That was a miracle. We also got to meet Jonathan's friends, see where he worked, and attend his Bible study and his church.

We were amazed at how God provided the whole trip so cheaply. This ended up being one of the cheapest vacations we had ever taken, and in the 2nd highest cost of living state in the country, no less! The airfare was donated by Andy and Audrey (free airfare), we stayed with Jonathan (free lodging), and he let us use his car that he was about to sell (free rental car).

Side story: Jonathan had recently bought a truck, but hadn't sold his car yet; so he put his car back on his auto insurance for the week that we were there, and it only cost $6.00! A week long rental car that only cost $6.00. Only God could arrange that.

However, we did splurge on a day cruise in Seward in Resurrection Bay for our anniversary. That was amazing! It was a beautiful sunny day with deep blue skies and puffy white clouds. We saw mountains and glaciers and whales and eagles and on and on. What an unbelievable gift from God as we were coming out of a dark valley.

After we returned home, we put some of our Alaska pictures on Facebook. I found out later that this really encouraged other cancer patients. This showed them that they could get back into life after cancer treatment too.

Our trip was almost exactly one year after I finished chemotherapy treatments. Even though I was not nearly back to normal yet, I could still do so much. I had begun to wonder if I would ever be able to do normal things again, because chemo, radiation and surgeries had taken such a toll on my body; but after returning home, I felt like this trip showed me that I really was getting back to normal. God used this trip not only to help us see our son and see Alaska, but to give me and other cancer patients hope and encouragement for the future.

Jonathan, Marcia and Dave Hiking On
A Glacier In Alaska, July 2014.

Pray About Everything?

Marcia:

One side effect from my chemo treatments was the development of neuropathy, which resulted in a painful burning sensation in my feet. It was annoying, since it meant that I couldn't be on my feet for long periods of time. I would do things around the house and then be forced to prop my feet up on the couch to get some relief. Then I would get up and do more things around the house, and then head back to the couch.... This neuropathy also kept me from falling asleep at night unless I took pain medication first.

Well, this went on for a while until one day when God urged me to pray about this. I really didn't want to, because I knew there were so many people who have to deal with much worse things than this. What was I looking for? A perfect life? I would feel so selfish if I asked for this pain to disappear.

Then the Lord reminded me of Philippians 4:6 which says, "Be anxious for nothing, but in *everything* by prayer and supplication with thanksgiving, *let your requests be made known to God.*" (NASB) I had to admit that the pain in my feet was included in the category of "everything", so I began to pray for my feet.

I am humbled to say that God answered my prayer. The neuropathy didn't go away, but it did get significantly better. I still have neuropathy today, but it is extremely mild in comparison to what it was then. I am still learning to take everything to God in prayer. I think I will be learning this lesson my whole life.

Camp

Marcia:

When this neuropathy had been at its worst point, I began to wonder if I could still cook out at our church camp. I absolutely love to cook, and God had called me to use this passion for cooking at a week-long camp every summer. God had made it clear to me that if I would fill the kid's stomachs, He would fill their souls. It is hard work, as we are on our feet from about 6:30 a.m. to about 8:30 p.m., cooking for about one hundred people in a hot kitchen with no air conditioning.

I took off the year that I was undergoing chemo and radiation of course, but was told (jokingly) that the camp would only give me one year off! It had been difficult for the camp to find a replacement cook.

The following year I was itching to cook at camp again, but I had serious doubts that I would be physically up to it, as my strength and energy were only about 50% back to normal at best. And that awful neuropathy! How in the world could I be on my feet all day when at home I could only be on my feet for about twenty minutes at a time before resting them? I began to pray for a miracle. I stepped out in faith and told the camp that I would cook again that year. I prayed so much ahead of time, for my feet, for strength, for energy, and for a large competent kitchen staff (since it's always volunteer help).

When camp started, I was amazed to have three full time women there all week, and many others who came and went. I have never had three full time workers--ever! They were so great! I think they could have run the kitchen all week without me. They were sympathetic about my feet and my weakened state, and often told me to go sit in a recliner and rest.

The most amazing part was that God answered my prayer and gave my feet relief. From the beginning of the week to the end of the week, I barely felt my neuropathy. The next week when camp was over, the neuropathy came back in full. This was proof that God had provided the miracle that I had prayed for. God is amazing!

A New Lump

Marcia:

About a year and a half after my diagnosis, when I was all finished with chemo, radiation, and most of my surgeries, I felt a new lump. I asked Dave if I was just imagining this or not. He said I was not. He said that I needed to get this lump checked out right away. I discovered it on a Wednesday. On Thursday I called my cancer center. My doctor was booked up on Friday, but wanted to see me on Monday.

I had enjoyed amazing peace since the beginning of my diagnosis, but now I was starting to get worried. Had the cancer come back? The lump was between my left breast and my armpit. All I could think of was that cancer was now in my lymph nodes. Not good. Not good. Not good.

On Thursday, Dave said that maybe we should tell some people. I said why? We didn't have any facts to tell them. On Friday, Dave again said that maybe we should tell some people. I again said no, because we didn't have anything concrete to tell them. I especially didn't want to alarm my side of the family since they have already been through so many cancer related tragedies. So we told no one.

By Friday night, I was consumed with worry. I was a mess! I was so scared that I was curled up on the living room floor sobbing. Dave just picked me up and held me in his arms and prayed for me. Where was that awesome peace that had carried me all the way through my cancer adventure?

On Saturday, I spent most of the afternoon in the kitchen preparing dinner for guests that night. I had our iPad reading the

Psalms out loud, and I listened to one Psalm after another while I cooked. I could feel the Lord quieting my heart.

Then one verse jumped out at me. I don't even remember the chapter or the verse, or even what the verse was talking about, but one word pierced my heart. TOGETHER. I stopped cooking and just thought about this. God was helping me understand that we needed to share this concern with our spiritual family. We needed to go through this *together* with our brothers and sisters in Christ. We needed their prayers. I told Dave that he was right. I should have listened to him. We should share it. We should have shared it right away.

On Sunday morning before church, Dave shared it with his group of elders that meet for prayer. They prayed with him. I shared it with my pre-service prayer group. They prayed with me. We both shared it at a meeting we had after church, and again, they prayed with us.

By the time we got home, God had restored my peace. I was ok now. God had shown me what happens when there is no prayer cover. We are more vulnerable to attacks from Satan when no one is praying. I should have listened to my husband and shared it much sooner.

On Monday, I went to my cancer center. They did an ultrasound, but couldn't get a clear picture because of scar tissue. Then they did a biopsy, and took six samples to the lab. They asked me if I could spend the night in a hotel, so that the doctor could tell me the results the next day.

I went back the next day, and as I was sitting in the waiting room, I just marveled at the remarkable peace I had while I was waiting to see if I had cancer again. I was completely at peace if it had come back or if it hadn't come back.

Then my doctor came *running* out to see me with a big smile on her face. She said that the lab report showed no cancer cells present at all, and that it was just a buildup of scar tissue from several past surgeries in that area. She said that when she read the lab report in her office, she jumped up and did a happy dance! I was relieved, but my peace had been the same before and after the news. God had taught me a valuable lesson. We need each other. We need prayer cover.

Cancer Lessons

Marcia:

At one point, I felt the Lord telling me to write down the things I have learned through this cancer experience. Here are some of them:

1. We will not go through illnesses alone. God will be with us every step of the way. It was amazing how God would send me verses just when I needed it. At one point, when I felt like we were entering uncharted waters, God sent Isaiah 42:16 "I will lead the blind by a way they do not know, in paths they do not know I will guide them. I will make darkness into light before them and rugged places into plains. These are the things I will do, and I will not leave them undone." (NASB) This was the encouragement that I needed to know that God was right there with us, and to keep on trusting Him.

2. I need to reach out to others. Because I have been so wrapped up in myself most of my life, I have largely ignored others when they are going through illnesses. It's been a wake-up call for me to reach out to people during their trials and illnesses, even when I don't feel like it.

3. There are always people who have it worse than I do. I have *nothing* to complain about. For example, I have met or heard of: 1) a woman whose husband died suddenly in the middle of her chemo treatments, 2) a woman whose husband was

diagnosed with cancer six weeks after she was diagnosed with cancer, 3) a woman whose cancer had returned twice and who was going through chemotherapy for the third time. I must not complain. I must be thankful.

4.   I should pray about everything. (Philippians 4:6) I am still learning to take everything to God in prayer, whether it is a physical issue, or a spiritual issue, a large issue, or a small issue. God wants to hear it all.

5.   A secret weapon to use in this battle is thankfulness. I found that when I thanked God for this illness, and for all that this illness brings, then anger, bitterness, and depression can't take root. In their place, God sends contentment and peace. It sounds crazy to thank God for hard times, but if it brings contentment and peace, *then it is so worth it.*

6.   It is so easy to worship an illness. When you have a serious illness, your life is turned up-side down. You are immersed in it, trying to figure it out, trying to beat it. It is so easy to become focused on you alone, shutting out the world. You hear of others that are suffering too, but you choose to ignore them. God wants me to reach out to others in the midst of my own suffering. Jesus, in the midst of intense suffering on the cross, was thinking of others when he said, "Father, forgive them…." (Luke 23:34) I was at my cancer center one day, sitting in the pharmacy waiting for my prescription. I struck up a conversation with a woman sitting next to me. Her son had cancer, and she was so worried about him. I prayed with her, and afterwards she thanked me and said that that was just what she needed. I'm still learning….

7.   I need to be gracious to people. When you have an illness, you are constantly approached by people who genuinely

want to know how you are doing. (How are you doing? Are your treatments over? When is your next surgery? Can I do anything for you? Etc.) They mean well, but it gets old. This is especially exhausting for an introvert. I've often thought that an illness is one of my worst nightmares. I'd have to talk! Over and over and over. God has shown me that I need to extend grace to all these well meaning people. For goodness sake, I've been one of them for years! I've asked these same questions to many people, too. Do I want to be treated poorly? Of course not. I need to take the time to talk to people. They've been praying for me. I need to let them know about answered prayer and how I am really doing. This gives them encouragement and lets them know how to pray more specifically.

I also need to be gracious to people who tell me their story, or their cousin's story, or their co-worker's story......or who tell me to go to this doctor or that cancer center.....or try these vitamins.....or do or don't eat or drink such and such, etc. They all mean well. I should just smile and thank them, and say, "Thank you for telling me that. I'll keep that in mind." Oh, how I am still learning to be gracious.....

8. I need prayer cover. As I told the story earlier of keeping my concerns to myself, I need to open my mouth and let people know what I am dealing with. This helps raise up prayer. It is dangerous to travel this road alone.

Why Does God Allow Suffering?

Marcia:

As I continued through this illness of cancer, I began to see firsthand some of the reasons why God sends suffering. I felt God leading me to write them down and share them openly. This is not an exhaustive list, but it is a list of *some* of the reasons I've learned while going through cancer.

1. To show how God can bring good things out of hard times. God used my mom's battle with cancer to bring about my own spiritual awakening. These good things may not be tangible; in this case it was spiritual. In other instances, they were tangible. Hard times may happen for the benefit of other people.

2. To increase our dependence on God. Dave and I came to the Lord over and over again, asking for guidance, for provision, for strength, etc. God doesn't want us to try to handle it all by ourselves. He wants us to turn to Him first.

3. To show us God's glory and power. In John 9:3, Jesus answered, "It was neither that this man sinned, nor his parents; *but it was so that the works of God might be displayed in him*." (NASB) Even if we *see* nothing powerful in our circumstances, if all we do is just trust God through it all, that alone is a work of God's power in our lives. People are watching and will be encouraged to follow our example

when God brings hard times into their lives too. "If so and so can trust God, even when nothing is going right, I can trust Him too."

4. To equip us to help others who are going through the same trial. Now that I have battled cancer, I am much more able to reach out to other cancer patients than I could in the past. I know from experience what they are going through, and can truly say I understand, because I've also been there.

5. To possibly prepare us for a much larger ministry or a different ministry. I never would have thought about writing a book if I had not gone through cancer. I would have stayed in the shadows. I may never have stepped out of my comfort zone to face a much larger audience.

6. To humble us, reduce our pride, or protect us from becoming prideful. I heard a quote that got my attention. "Clouds of darkness are methods of grace to humble my soul." (Matthew Henry) It humbles us when our "perfect" life suddenly isn't perfect anymore. It hurts our pride, because people are watching. Humility is good for us, isn't it?! The apostle Paul was given a "thorn in the flesh" to keep him from becoming prideful.

2 Corinthians 12:7b (NLT)

"...So to keep me from becoming proud, I was given a thorn in the flesh, a messenger from Satan to torment me and keep me from becoming proud."

7. To teach us lessons. For example, I learned how much it means when people reached out to us with cards, phone calls, practical acts of service, and prayer. I needed to learn

to reach out to people as well. It has always been easy for me to just stay in the background and let others reach out and care for people who are going through hard times. I saw that I am lazy and self centered. I only did what felt good to me. I felt the Lord rebuking me, but I also sensed that He was encouraging me to change my ways and begin to reach out to others. Oh how I needed to learn this lesson.

8. To purify us. When gold or silver is heated to extremely high temperatures, the impurities float to the top and are discarded, and the remaining metal is pure. So it is with our lives. When trials come and the heat is turned up, our impurities come to the surface to be dealt with. We come out stronger and wiser. We grow so much closer to the Lord. We learn to surrender.

Dave and I have learned firsthand that when you go through trials, you grow at a much faster pace. The things we have learned have not always been easy. Sometimes they are painful. Afterwards, however, you see the beauty in it all.

Isaiah 48:10

"Behold, I have refined you, but not as silver; I have tested you in the furnace of affliction." (NASB)

1 Peter 5:10

"After you have suffered for a little while, the God of all grace, who called you to His eternal glory in Christ, will Himself perfect, confirm, and establish you." (NASB)

9. To test and solidify our trust in God. I'm beginning to think that the core reason for trials is to test and strengthen our trust in God.

    If you think about it, when life is going smoothly, I can easily say that I trust God. Then a trial appears, and now life is considerably harder. It may be a little harder now to say that I still trust God 100%. Then the trial intensifies, or more trials enter the picture on top of the first one, or the trial/trials go on and on, never ending. Now it is even harder than ever to say that I still trust God.

    I am now at a crossroads. I have to make a decision. Do I continue to trust God, when I'm barely hanging onto my faith, or do I say I've had enough and turn my back on God completely? Now it is time to ask myself a hard question. Is He only my God during the good times and not during the hard times? Is He only my God so that I can have a smooth life?

    Job 2:10b (NASB)

    "Shall we indeed accept good from God and not accept adversity?"

    God is not a mean God. He doesn't send trials just to make me miserable.

    Here are the facts:

    1.) God is love. (1John 4:8b NASB)

    2.) God never changes. (Malachi 3:6a NASB).

So, if God allows a trial/trials to come into my life, it is out of love; if I begin to lose my trust in God, then who has changed? Not God, because He never changes. He still loves me. He has not turned against me. Who has changed then? It is *I* who have changed.

I may think of love only in terms of giving good gifts, but trials can be extremely good gifts. If a trial in my life drives me to utter dependence upon God, then it is a good gift. If a trial in my life ends up helping other people, then it is a good gift. If a trial in my life helps purify my heart, then it is a good gift. If a trial in my life strengthens my trust in God, then it is a good gift.

James 1:3

....knowing that the testing of your faith produces endurance.(NASB)

1 Peter 1:7 (TLB)

These trials are only to test your faith, to see whether or not it is strong and pure. It is being tested as fire tests gold and purifies it—and your faith is far more precious to God than mere gold; so if your faith remains strong after being tried in the test tube of fiery trials, it will bring you much praise and glory and honor on the day of His return.

Do I Really Hear God's Voice?

Marcia:

Throughout this book, I have said, "I heard God speak to me, not audibly, but in my heart….." Maybe you are wondering how I can hear Him so clearly. The only way I know how to explain this is to share more of my life story.

My parents took my family to church every Sunday for as long as I can remember. When I was about ten years old, we started attending a new church. That's when I became aware that something was different with my parents. They had already been Christians, but now they were excited about serving the Lord. Now they had a hunger to read the Bible and pray. This made me very much aware that I was *not* a Christian.

This became even clearer to me when our church played a movie called *A Thief in the Night*. This movie showed what would happen when Jesus came down to earth, gathered up everyone who was a Christian, and took them up to heaven during His second coming to Earth, which many people call the *rapture*. Boy oh boy, did that scare me! Suddenly I knew that when that actually happens, my parents would instantly disappear, because they were Christians. The thought of living in this world without my parents terrified me! How could a ten year old live without parents? I wouldn't be able to support myself financially or drive a car or do a thousand other adult things. For a while I lived with this paralyzing fear.

One day when I was upstairs in my bedroom, I could hear my mom in the kitchen stirring something on the stove; then there was silence. My heart pounded. Had she been raptured? I quietly sneaked down the stairs, peeked around the corner, and saw that she was still there. Whew! What sweet relief! Then this happened again. Silence. Sneek. Peek. Relief! The third time it happened, my mom saw me peeking around the corner and asked me what I was doing. I burst into tears, and it all spilled out. She said, "Marcia, you can become a Christian too." I told her that I didn't know how.

She took me to her bedroom and explained how. She led me through a small booklet. This showed me that no sin is allowed in Heaven. Since everyone is a sinner, then no one is allowed into Heaven. That included me, too.

Even as a ten year old, I knew I was a sinner. I was selfish. I could see this when I played with my brother and sisters. I lied to my parents now and then, especially in the form of exaggerating the truth. I had really mean thoughts toward difficult people, like my teacher at school. I had clashed with a neighborhood friend and refused to reconcile with her. Oh I knew I was a sinner. Since sinners can't get into heaven, now it seemed like *I* could never get into Heaven.

My mom went on to explain that no one can ever earn their way to Heaven. No one can ever do enough good things in their life to get into Heaven. God even says in the Bible that all of our good deeds (our efforts) are like filthy rags in His sight. (Isaiah 64:6 NIV) He is offended by them. He doesn't want us to try to get to heaven by our own efforts. For example, if you gave an extremely valuable gift to a friend, and then they spent the rest of their lives trying to pay you for it, you would be offended first of all by their refusal to just accept it as a gift, and secondly by the payments they gave you over the years. The payments would constantly irritate you.

There is only one way that it is possible for sinners to get into Heaven. Someone who had never sinned could voluntarily die for sinners and trade places with them. My mom told me that Jesus was the only person who had never sinned. He loved us so much that He left Heaven, came to Earth, and died a horrible death on a cross in our place so that all sinners who believe in Him could go to Heaven. He had traded His perfect life with us sinners, and took on all of our sins.

She asked me if I believed that Jesus did this for me. I said yes. She then asked me if I wanted to ask Jesus to come into my heart. I desperately wanted to, but it felt like there was a battle going on and something was trying to prevent me from doing it. With all my strength, I went against this force and said yes. I asked Jesus to come into my heart that day. Instantly I had peace. All my worries disappeared. I felt like a brand new person. I was now a Christian and had complete confidence that I would go to Heaven some day.

Over the next few years, I learned that just as food is needed for the human body to function properly, so the Bible is needed in a Christian's life to function properly. The Bible is our spiritual food. Without spending time daily with my Savior by reading His words in the Bible and praying with Him, I would be spiritually malnourished, like a spiritually emaciated person, with only skin and bones walking around. This is so dangerous and unhealthy.

The Bible tells us that we must spend time with Christ continuously. This is illustrated in John 15:4-5 which I have paraphrased in my own words: "Stay connected to Me (Jesus), and I will stay connected to you. Just as a branch cannot produce fruit all by itself unless it is connected to the vine, so you also cannot produce fruit unless you stay connected to Me. I am the vine, and you are the branches; anyone who is connected to Me and I to him will produce much fruit, because if you are not connected to Me, you can produce nothing."

During the next few years, I would try to read the Bible, but I was terribly inconsistent. I would read it for a few days, and then end up skipping it for a few months. Satan was constantly making me feel guilty about this. I was so frustrated! I just couldn't do it.

Then a significant thing happened during a New Year's Eve party at our youth group at church one year. One of our youth leaders challenged us to spend an entire year without missing a single quiet time. He told us to make it our new year's resolution to spend time with God every day, reading the Bible and praying. I thought–whoa! A whole year? Is that really possible? Hmmm. Intriguing. I decided to take the challenge, although I told no one for fear that I would fail. Do you know what? I had a quiet time every day until the middle of summer. Then the Holy Spirit impressed upon me that God was not angry with me. Then I knew He still loved me. I started up again and kept going. That helped me conquer inconsistency. I still miss now and then, but I just pick it up again and keep going.

Then my mom was diagnosed with cancer, and you know that part (ch.3-- An Important Lesson). I developed a hunger for the Bible then. When I would spend time reading the Bible and pouring my heart out to Jesus, I began to hear His voice in my heart.

There is a direct connection here. The more time I spend with the Lord, the more I hear His voice. If I don't spend time with Him, He seems distant. Has *He* really become distant, or am *I* the one who has become distant?

When I have my quiet time in the morning, I picture Him sitting in the rocking chair across the room. I open my Bible and ask Him to speak to me. I hear Him then in my heart, as well as throughout the day. Having my quiet time every day is not a duty to perform. It is a daily opportunity to continue developing a close relationship with the God of all existence who created me and loves me.

I read a booklet once that described how God *wants* to spend time with me each day. He longs for and enjoys my company. For a long time I had been having quiet times without God. I was just going through the motions, like it was something to check off on my to-do list. It really didn't mean much to me. Now I picture Him in the room with me, and I can feel his loving presence. It's like spending time with a really good friend, except that He is so much more than that. He is the source of love. He is the source of wisdom. He constantly forgives me when I fail. His love just never stops! He cares about every part of my life, and absolutely loves it when I include Him in every part. Can I really hear His voice? Yes, but it's a still small voice in my heart. I have to be spending time with Him, and I have to be listening.

Here's an example of hearing His voice. One day, I was out running errands. I was approaching a busy intersection and needed to turn left. I looked down to turn on the turn signal, but I couldn't find it. The closer I got to the intersection, the faster my heart was beating, because I just could not figure out where the turn signal was! It was where it had always been, of course, right in front of me on the steering wheel. I was experiencing the peak of "chemo brain" and could not make my brain work when I needed it to. I cried out and said, "Jesus, help me!" Right then I felt Him directing me to just go home, so I turned right and safely went home, even though I wasn't finished with my errands. Who knows what other unsafe things I might have done if I hadn't listened? It was just as if He was sitting right next to me in the car, and wisely answered me when I cried out.

However, there's more to it than just hearing God's voice in my heart. Once I've heard Him speak, then I have the responsibility to obey Him. It may go against what I want to do, but it is always best.

John 10:4b (NASB)

....and the sheep follow Him because they know His voice.

The Hunger Dream

Marcia:

When I was at my cancer center recovering from the big ten hour surgery, my doctor told us to stay in a nearby hotel over the weekend, so that he could see me one more time before I went home, as I mentioned earlier; but while we were in the hotel, something unusual happened.

As we were getting ready for bed, I realized that I was *really* hungry. I had eaten a normal dinner, so I told myself to just ignore it and go to bed. In the middle of the night, I woke up *extremely* hungry. I mean, *very uncomfortably* hungry. I kept thinking that I should get up and eat something, but it was so hard to get up with fresh incisions, so I didn't. But this *intense* hunger wouldn't let me sleep! Then I remembered that it was time to take my pain medication, and I wasn't supposed to take it on an empty stomach. Hallelujah! Now I had a solid reason to get up and eat something and get rid of this *awful, gnawing* hunger! So with much effort, I got up and ate *a lot* of crackers to make sure it was gone. Then I went back to sleep.

A while later, I woke up again with this *horrible, consuming* hunger. What in the world was going on? I'd never had *unbearable* hunger like this before. Then I suddenly sucked in my breath and said, "Lord, if you are trying to tell me something, I'm listening." I waited in silence. Then I sensed the Lord speaking to me—not in an audible voice—but in my heart. He revealed to me that He was about to give me intense spiritual hunger. He was giving me a new ministry. I would need to prepare like an athlete prepares for an event. Then, as I laid there in silence, I said, "Lord, can I ask a question? Can you give my husband this same spiritual hunger so that we can both be on the same level?" He confirmed that this would happen. He also informed me that people will listen. Eventually I went back to sleep. In the morning I told Dave all about this over a hearty breakfast!

After that, as time went on, I waited for answers. What was this new ministry? How was I supposed to prepare? I didn't get any answers. I talked to my friend Nancy, and told her about this "hunger dream." (I call this a "dream" because I don't know what else to call it.) I asked her what should I do now? She said to just keep doing what I am already doing until the Lord gives me answers. Keep reading His word and praying daily, and keep doing the ministries He had already called me to. So I did.

Eventually the Lord directed me to start doing one thing. I was to read the book of John (in the Bible), and write it out in my own words. At first it sounded easy, but then I realized how long it would take. Every time I came to something that I didn't understand (which was often), I would have to stop and look it up in commentaries. Sometimes I would ask Dave and other Bible scholars what they thought it meant. Sometimes I just could not figure out how to write it in my own words, and would look up other versions to see how it was worded.

This took about a year. It slowed my Bible reading way down. I couldn't move on until I understood it. I got so much more out of my quiet times by doing this. There were a few times when it became almost mechanical, just an exercise to complete. Then I realized that each time, I needed to look across the room to the chair that I envisioned Jesus sitting in and say, "Lord, open my heart. I want to hear from *You* today." Then the passage would come alive and Jesus would speak to me right where I was.

About six months after the "hunger dream," I came before the Lord and said that I still didn't know what else to do to prepare. Should I memorize passages? Should I pray for long periods of time on a regular basis? Should I start fasting? What? And what is this new ministry? I began to be frustrated with no answers. Was that "hunger dream" really real? Did I just imagine it? Dave assured me that it was real, but I still had no answers. So I just kept writing the book of John in my own words and continuing on as always.

Reason for Cancer?

Marcia:

Earlier in the spring, Dave and I drove down to Mississippi to visit our daughter in college. We had a great time with her. On the drive back home, we decided to have our quiet times together in the car. I started reading out loud in John chapter 9, and read about the man who was born blind. The disciples asked Jesus who had sinned, this man or his parents, that caused his blindness? Jesus answered, "It was neither that this man sinned, nor his parents; but it was so that the works of God might be displayed in him. We must work the works of Him who sent Me as long as it is day. Night is coming when no one can work." John 9:3-4 (NASB) A shiver ran down our backs. Dave and I just looked at each other in awe. We knew that God was speaking to our hearts. This was one of the reasons that I was given cancer! God wanted to display His powerful works in our lives! Now more than ever, God wanted us to tell people what He had done in our lives through cancer.

As Dave began to tell his customers at work, they really listened! And every time I went to my cancer center, I would strike up conversations with people in waiting rooms and in the cafeteria. I would listen to their story, and then they would ask me about mine. Then I would tell them how God had done amazing things in our lives. This was a ministry that we had not expected. It was pretty easy, actually. Was this the ministry that God meant in the "hunger dream?" I still didn't know.

Now it was a year after I had experienced the "hunger dream." I was embarrassed because I had told several people about this dream, and I now felt like I had nothing to show for it. I felt like they were watching me to see what would happen, and nothing was happening. Was anything ever going to happen?

At this time, we were going through the book "Experiencing God" by Henry and Richard Blackaby in Sunday school. One chapter really spoke to me and calmed my frustrations. It said, "He (God) may spend years preparing your character or developing your love relationship with Him before He gives you a large assignment. Don't get discouraged if the task or "call" does not come immediately. Remain faithful in what He has told you to do, no matter how small or seemingly insignificant it may appear. God knows what He is doing. Focus on deepening your communion with God, and out of that fellowship will inevitably flow effective service for God. ...Be patient and learn to trust Him. God will first build some basic foundations into your life before He gives you a larger role in service to Him." (Experiencing God; Knowing and Doing the Will of God, by Henry and Richard Blackaby with Claude King, p.121— revised and expanded edition) And again I heard His voice a few chapters later: "If you have not received instructions from God on a matter, pray and wait. Learn patience. Depend on God's timing, for His agenda is always best. Don't be in a hurry. Don't try to skip over the relationship to get on with the activity." (Experiencing God; Knowing and Doing the Will of God, by Henry and Richard Blackaby, with Claude King, p.151, revised and expanded edition) This is what my frustrated heart needed to hear. God needed to work on my character while I waited, and I needed to learn patience while waiting for God's timing.

What Should I Do Next?

Marcia:

One day when I was having my quiet time, I asked the Lord what He wanted me to do next. I felt God directing me to go out to the local Christian school and speak in their chapel about the powerful things He has done in our lives through cancer. "What? Me? Lord, I don't know how to relate to high school kids!" Right then several thoughts came to my mind about how I could word things in a way that would be on their level. Now I knew what God wanted me to do, at least for a short term assignment. I called the principal and told her what I heard the Lord say to me. She said that she would talk to the pastor who was in charge of the chapels and get back to me.

The next Sunday in church, she came up to me and said that there was an unexpected opening this Friday. Could I come then? Uh, really? That soon? I guess I really am doing this! I spent a lot of time praying as I prepared my talk.

Then the day came, and I spoke in chapel. It went very smoothly. All of the kids kept eye contact with me all the way through, and no one fell asleep! Afterwards, one of the staff members came up to me and told me an amazing story about how God had saved one of their children after an accident. Then one of the students came up to me and told me about a trial that she had gone through in her life and how the Lord taught her through it.

Right then, I learned that I should eagerly listen to the stories of how the Lord has worked in the lives of others, and not just focus on what He is doing in my life. I'm so self centered that God had to teach me how to look at what He is doing in the lives of others.

I continued to ask the Lord what I should do next. I said, "Lord, I'm available. Use me." I have since found out that when you say that, you better buckle your seat belt. I was thinking what *short term* thing should I do next. That was not what the Lord had in mind!

One day, not too long after that, I was having my quiet time. I didn't understand a verse I was reading, so I went online to look up the verse in other translations. I went to biblegateway.com, and suddenly a side-bar ad jumped out at me. It said, "Share your story. Publish your book. Free guide."

Now over the last two years as I've told people about the amazing works of God in our lives through cancer, I've heard several people say, "You should write a book about your cancer adventure." Uh huh. Right. I would totally ignore this and move on. I am an introvert, and writing a book is the last thing I want to do. I value my privacy. I don't want to bare it all. So I did nothing—until I saw that small side-bar ad.

Now when I saw that ad, my thoughts came to a screeching halt. I could think of nothing else. It was like a neon sign was flashing in front of my face saying, "Write a book! Write a book! Write a book!" I felt that the Lord was speaking directly to my heart and was showing me that I had been ignoring His gentle nudging. Now He had put it right in front of my eyes.

At the beginning when I was diagnosed with cancer, I had told the Lord, "The way I see it, You created me which means You own me; therefore, You can do anything You want with my body." It was relatively easy to let the Lord have full control of my physical body, but now He was asking for full control of my lips? Ohhhhh dear. This is really hard to let go of. I DON'T WANT TO GO PUBLIC! I like being behind the scenes! However, I've learned that it's just not worth it to rebel against the Lord.

So with great fear and trembling, I filled out the information to just "get the free guide," and my toes curled as I forced myself

to click "send". I told myself that I'm not signing up for anything-
-I'm just asking for information. No commitment. This should be
"safe". Well, two days later, I got a call from a publishing consultant.
Gulp—here we go!! That is how this book started. I used many of
the stories from my journal that I had entitled "Book of Miracles."
Now that I look back on it, that title was kind of prophetic, wasn't it?

Then God reminded me of all the verses that He had sent to
Dave and I throughout our cancer adventure that seemed to have a
recurring theme: *Tell of His works in our lives.* Throughout our cancer
adventure, these are the verses that God sent to us with that theme:

Psalm 35:18 & 28 (NASB)

> *I will give You thanks in the great congregation. I
> will praise You among a mighty throng. V.28 And
> my tongue shall declare Your righteousness and Your
> praise all day long.*

Psalm 34:1-2 (NASB)

> I will bless the Lord at all times. His praise shall
> continually be in my mouth. *My soul will make its
> boast in the Lord. The humble shall hear it and rejoice.*

Psalm 66:16 (NASB)

> Come and hear, all who fear God, and *I will tell of
> what He has done for my soul.*

Psalm 78:4 (NASB)

> We will not conceal them from their children, but
> *tell to the generation to come the praises of the Lord,*

*and His strength and His wondrous works that He
has done.*

Psalm 89:1(NASB)

I will sing of the loving kindness of the Lord forever;
*To all generations I will make known Your faithfulness
with my mouth.*

Who was I to resist this new assignment?

As I started to write this book, Satan began to attack.
Discouraging thoughts started filling my mind. *"What in the world
am I doing?! I don't know how to write a book! I can't do this. I will
never have enough words to fill a book. No one will ever want to read
a book from a quiet homemaker in a small town. Another cancer story?
There are so many out there already!"*

One evening when my husband and I were washing dishes, he
turned on some music. The words to a song arrested my thoughts.
I stopped washing dishes, put my head down on the sink, and just
listened to all the words. I felt like the Lord sent it just for me.

The song talked about having faith to walk on water, and having
faith to fight a giant. It encouraged us to step out of our comfort
zones to follow Jesus. It said not to listen to the enemy who whispers
that you can't do it. Jesus instead encourages us not to be afraid,
because this is for His glory. I knew then that all those discouraging
thoughts were from Satan. I have to choose not to believe them.
Writing *Pink Ribbon Adventure* is for God's glory, to show the
powerful works of God in our lives in the midst of breast cancer.

Acknowledgements

There are so many people I would like to thank that I hardly know where to begin! My husband Dave was the first person I told about the idea of this book. He came on board literally overnight, and has been my constant help. Thank you, Dave, for your wisdom and sharp insight. I am so blessed to have you write from a husband's perspective. I'm so glad we went through this adventure together!

Eric Schroeder, the publishing consultant from WestBow Press, was the next person to come on the scene and was so incredibly patient with me. Every phone call was filled with encouragement from him. Thanks for all you have done, Eric.

Hannah, my heart bled when I read your part of the book. I know it wasn't easy to relive all that you experienced during this adventure. I am truly thankful that you volunteered to write in this book. I think we all grew while writing it. Thank you for opening up your heart.

Nancy Kerr, you don't know how much I have valued your advice! You were the first one to read the manuscript outside of ourselves, and your wise discernment that this book idea was from God helped us go forward with it.

To all twelve ladies on the prayer team for this book, thank you a million times over! You faithfully prayed for this book from start to finish. Many prayers were answered because of you. I felt like the Lord held all of us in His hands during this whole time because you were faithfully praying. You all are precious. May God bless you!

Thank you Andy and Audrey Minch, Nancy Kerr, and Leslie

Davidson for all the unpaid editing and work you did for us. This was such a big help! You all were such a blessing from God.

The highest thanks and praise of all goes to the true author of this book, Jesus Christ. He initiated it, and He authored it. I was merely the pen that He used to write it down. Thank you Jesus for showing how You are present during every trial, loving us, teaching us, humbling us, guiding us, and blessing us. Praise you, Jesus. You are good, all the time.

Personal Note

There were so many times when I felt so unqualified to write this book. Time and time again, I felt like I hadn't experienced the depth of suffering that many people have endured. I honestly feel like I have not even begun to experience the overwhelming physical and emotional agony of crushing ongoing difficulties and trials that so many people face. There are many people who are much more experienced and qualified to speak about suffering than myself. I said more than once, "God, are you sure you want *me* to write this book?" He replied that a person doesn't have to experience every kind of suffering at every level in order to tell about His power and love. In the end, it always came back to the fact that my Commander had given me an assignment, and it was my responsibility to carry it out. He has done so much for me. It is now my privilege to do this for Him.

About the Author

Marcia DeVries is a homemaker and a breast cancer survivor. She and her husband Dave live in Dixon, Illinois. They have two grown children, Jonathan (and his wonderful wife Amy), who live in Anchorage, Alaska, and Hannah, who lives in Mississippi. Marcia received cancer treatment at Cancer Treatment Centers of America in Zion, Illinois. She sees herself as a soldier awaiting assignments from her Spiritual Commander each day.

They can be reached at pradventure13@gmail.com.

Printed in the United States
By Bookmasters